NO HOLDING BACK

MICHAEL HOLDING

WITH EDWARD HAWKINS

NO HOLDING BACK

Weidenfeld & Nicolson
LONDON

First published in Great Britain in 2010
by Weidenfeld & Nicolson

1 3 5 7 9 10 8 6 4 2

Text © Michael Holding 2010

A CIP catalogue record for this book
is available from the British Library.

HB ISBN-13 978 0 297 85935 2
TPB ISBN-13 978 0 297 85936 9

Typeset by Input Data Services Ltd,
Bridgwater, Somerset

Printed and bound in the UK
by CPI Mackays, Chatham, Kent

The Orion Publishing Group's policy is to use papers that
are natural, renewable and recyclable products and made
from wood grown in sustainable forests. The logging and
manufacturing processes are expected to conform to
the environmental regulations of the country of origin.

CONTENTS

1

THE MAKING OF WHISPERING DEATH

I cannot have been far off my seventh birthday when on a December night I wriggled into bed between my mother and father, seeking comfort and pretending to be interested in the crackle and wheeze of the transistor radio concealed in the bed head. They were listening to coverage of the West Indies' tour of Australia in 1960–61. I was asleep long before I knew who was actually batting. I had little interest or understanding of what the commentators were explaining, but looking back on that wonderful memory, it brings a smile to my face to think of what life had in store.

My childhood was full of such happy times. I grew up at 29 Dunrobin Avenue in Kingston, Jamaica, the fourth and youngest child of Ralph and Enid. My mum and dad met at Kingston Parish Church. Mum was in the choir and Dad was an altar boy. It was a religious household and every Sunday we would be up early for church.

Sport was something of a religion for the Holdings, too. Mum did athletics and table tennis and Dad, who was a building contractor, loved his football, although cricket ran it a close second. In fact, I was only a few days old when he registered me as a member of the famous Melbourne Cricket Club, tucked away in a quiet corner of Kingston, which provided and continues to provide players for both Jamaica and the West Indies cricket teams. He captained the club's Minor Cup side, which was used to blood youngsters, and later in life he became president. My eldest sister Rheima competed in high jump in the inter-secondary school championships and Marjorie ran at the inter-collegiate championships representing the University of the West Indies, but neither would claim to have excelled; it was participation that mattered. Ralph Junior, who is five years older than me, loved his sports too, but was more of a musician. While he was at school (Kingston College, the same one my dad and later I attended), he sang in the choir and was lead treble on a few records that the school put out. He ended up living in Germany for about 15 years, touring Europe with a band and recording music, but then moved back home in the early 1990s and to this day continues, albeit part-time, in the music field, sometimes performing at the various north coast hotels in Jamaica.

My sporting life began in the gullies, woodland and scrubland that surrounded Dunrobin Avenue, which was a small residential area and completely underdeveloped, not like the bustling commercial centre it is today. Our old house is now an industrial complex and there are very few residences left on the road.

Behind that house in the wide open spaces, I played football, cricket or marbles and would go into the woods to shoot birds with homemade slingshots – anything which would get me out of the house.

As soon as I'd had my breakfast, I was outside playing. I was active, perhaps too active for my mother's liking. I was diagnosed with asthma when I was about three years old and had to carry an inhaler around with me everywhere I went. My mum and dad would always warn me not to overdo it. I'm sure a few international batsmen will scoff when they read that Michael Holding had asthma, in fact one day the asthma just disappeared and I haven't needed that inhaler since I was an early teenager.

I got into scrapes with my mum and dad because of my love of disappearing outdoors for the day. Often I would choose a day of running around with friends instead of cricket at Sabina Park on a Saturday. Sacrilege, I know. A day at Sabina was a big deal then, a real family affair. The Friday night before the match, everyone would be busy cooking rice, peas and chicken to take to the game but come Saturday morning, I would get up early and disappear before I could be dragged along. In the 1960s and early 70s, the seating in the South Western stand where my family sat wasn't that luxurious, and rather than sit and fidget in the same uncomfortable seat for six or seven hours, I preferred to play cricket myself.

This independence would come at a cost, though. I knew when Mum and Dad got home there would be a scolding, sometimes a beating too. It wasn't because they were afraid of what might happen to me (there were no such fears about letting kids run loose like there are today), but more to do with the fact that I hadn't sought their permission to do my own thing. I can still remember being out in the gully until darkness, losing track of time because I was having so much fun, and hearing Mum shout my name from the back fence to come in.

I didn't grow up in a rich household, but I got everything that I needed, rather than what I wanted. This way of living was something instilled in me from a young age: need, not want.

Just up the road from us lived the Blake family. Evon Blake was a respected businessman in Jamaica and he was, to put it diplomatically, more financially stable than we were. Both families were friendly and I was friends with the son, Paul. Paul got what he needed and probably wanted, too. Paul had bicycles. Note the plural. One day I borrowed one of his bikes and we were cycling down Dunrobin Avenue and unbeknown to me, Mum and Dad drove past us. Later on, Mum wanted to know why I was riding Paul's bike. My excuse was that I didn't have one of my own and Paul was happy to lend me one of his.

'If you don't have it, you can do without it,' Mum said. 'What if you had damaged it? You would have to replace it and you still wouldn't have one.' She was teaching me to live within my means.

When I was not riding other people's bikes, I was out in the gully playing sport, especially cricket, a form of the game in Jamaica that was called Catchy Shubby. Catchy Shubby could be described as organised chaos. It was the sort of free-for-all game played by scores of kids and grown men where the first one to turn up with a bat batted and when that person was out, it was the turn of the person who dismissed him to bat. While we obviously only had one batsman at a time, there could be four or five balls available to be bowled at him.

The ball was made of twine wrapped tightly around a hard core, then covered with layers of some form of cork seemingly mixed with a black tar-looking substance and painted red (proper leather cricket balls were too expensive and didn't last long enough for our budget). It would not take long before that red paint would get chipped away and we would be playing with a black ball that we all referred to as a cork and tar ball. There was a shopkeeper who we only knew by the name of Mr Mattis, whose store overlooked our playing area, and every now and again he would send one of his sons down the hill with a brand new red cricket ball. It was heaven. I think Mr Mattis enjoyed what he saw happening on the field and wanted to encourage us youngsters. Of course his kids took part at times, but that had nothing to do with his generosity.

The 'stumps' were a sheet of corrugated iron. They needed to make a good loud noise when the ball hit them so the batsman would not be able to deny that he was out. Without umpires, you can well understand why being bowled needed to be indisputable; there were no lbws, caught behinds were a rarity, too, and thin edges were hardly ever owned up to. If a batsman was out caught, it was the fielder taking the catch who would next get to bat, not the bowler. As a bowler, there was no point in trying to deceive the batsman with a beautiful slower ball so he might miscue into the hands of mid-off. I worked out that if I wanted to bat, I would have to bowl people out. Ping the zinc if you like. However, it was not easy because with no leg before, batsmen would cover the 'stumps' with their legs and if they were hit in front, it didn't matter.

The solution was to bowl so fast that if they got their legs in the way, that cork and tar ball would really sting. The next time they saw me running in, they wouldn't be so keen to get their legs in the way. They would remember the pain. It wasn't a case of blood on the pitch, but I suppose you could say that in those early games I discovered that I had the 'nasty' streak that was so important to becoming a successful fast bowler later in life, but also vital for the immediate prospects of getting to bat!

If that was when I developed the fast bowler 'attitude', the relaxed run-up for which I was known during my playing days would come later. In these early informal skirmishes, I had to bowl off a few steps because if you took a long run, there would be about four or five others who would sneak in front and bowl instead; no one was going to stand by and wait for you to run in from the next county. It was a skill that stayed with me through my Test career; I was often capable of generating good pace off just a couple of yards.

I couldn't have been more than ten when I played my first proper game of cricket. And when I say proper, I'm talking about players in whites with two umpires and an official start time. It was at Red Hills Oval on Red Hills Road, which led to the hills above Kingston, in a competition called the Rankine Cup. The cup was a competition for community and business teams. I was in the Dunrobin area team as an off-spin bowler who could bat a bit. At that age I was not strong enough to be bowling fast against men in those sorts of matches, even if I had played against adults in the gully. Besides, I enjoyed bowling offbreaks.

It was from playing against adults that I came to be picked for the Dunrobin team. They had seen that I was a useful player and invited me to have a game. As soon as I found out I was playing I went home and told my family. The problem was, I didn't have any kit so my sister Marjorie took me to the nearest shopping centre to buy some white pants. They weren't cricketing pants, just dress pants which we bought in a men's clothing store.

I was only a little boy playing against men in that first Rankine Cup game. It was intimidating. At the time, everyone in Jamaica used to go by nicknames rather than first or surnames, and I remember a man called 'Nixy', who was almost a local celebrity because of the weight of runs he would always score in that competition. He was very powerful, would hit the ball tremendously hard and he towered over me. He was probably only 5ft 9in, but with me being only 10, he seemed 6ft 10in and the thought of bowling to him was terrifying.

Those early formative days at the Red Hills Oval were unforgettable and great fun. That 'little ground' on the edge of Sandy Gully helped to shape the careers of Carlton Baugh Senior who played for Jamaica, Nehemiah Perry who played both for Jamaica and the West Indies and, of course, myself. Nehemiah came later though, as Carlton and myself played with his dad.

I progressed to playing most of my cricket for Melbourne in informal matches on Sundays when the club toured the rural areas of Jamaica. They were called Curry Goat matches because a goat or two was killed for lunch, and man, do I still love those goat curries. I would get the occasional game with Melbourne, whose senior members thought I had some ability and they wanted me to learn.

Dad had also spotted that I had a particular talent for cricket so he arranged for Teddy Griffith, son of the famous Barbadian and West Indian fast bowler Herman, and a Melbourne member and friend of the family, to give me some coaching. Herman Griffith's claim to fame was that he once bowled Donald Bradman for a duck in Sydney in 1931, the second Test won by the West Indies.

Personally, I didn't think I was particularly good or particularly bad. I just played for fun. That was the attitude I had to all sports, whether it be football or athletics. I just loved sport. I lived for it.

You often hear professional sportsmen say 'This is a dream come true' when they achieve recognition, but when I was young I didn't dream about playing cricket for Jamaica and I certainly didn't lie in bed at night and hope that I would one day bowl fast for West Indies. Nor did I look at players who were representing Jamaica or West Indies and think 'I want to be just like him'. It was never a goal of mine to play at the highest level of a sport that I thought of as just a hobby. Perhaps this was a reason for my success. I never put myself under any pressure and was just doing it for the love of the game.

Others pushed and encouraged me though, and I am grateful. Bruce Wellington, a left-arm spinner who played for Jamaica and could have played for West Indies with more luck, and Arthur Barrett, another spinner who actually played Test cricket, were Melbourne members and they would help me a great deal, teaching me the basics of bowling, like how to grip the ball. The older I got, the more they passed on. It was little things like the positioning of the body and using the crease to confuse the batsman. There were also experienced captains that

I played under, like George Sterling and Ruddy Williams, who helped along the way.

Despite great advice from such experienced players, it was Mum who gave me the most useful tip. As a cricket fan she was always present at my games and saw the slip fielders repeatedly dropping catches off my bowling. She was the first person to ever face Whispering Death and pointed out that my natural action was for outswingers. She told me that if I wanted to get more batsmen out, I would have to get wickets leg before and bowled, and that meant I would have to develop an inswinger. I did as I was told, but again with the help of the two spin bowlers, Barrett in particular, who showed me the basics of that delivery.

By 1965 I was attending Kingston College High School, one of the most illustrious schools in the country. My dad and brother had also gone there. At first I didn't play much cricket at high school, though, just a bit for my form team. Athletics was something I enjoyed immensely and because I was happy just being involved in any sport, rather than concentrating on one, I tried everything, including hurdles, 400 metres and the high jump.

This leads me nicely onto the first myth-buster of this book. It is widely perceived that my languid run-up when bowling, which has been described as 'elegant' and 'malevolent stealth personified' (very flattering), was a product of my promise as a 400-metre runner. It makes a nice story but it is not true in the least. To this day I still tell people that it was a mistake but the response is usually that they think I'm just being modest. One gentleman went as far as to tell me, 'I saw you run for Jamaica.' I had to tell him politely that he was mistaken.

The myth was perpetuated by Tony Cozier, the famous West Indian broadcaster and journalist, who got me mixed up with a guy called Seymour Newman. Seymour and myself opened the bowling for Jamaica's Under-19 youth team in the regional tournament in 1971 and '72. He was quick – quicker than me, actually – and represented the country in athletics. He won silver in the 800 metres (880 yards in those days) of the 1978 Commonwealth Games in Alberta, Canada, and was first to beat the great Cuban 400 metres (440 yards) runner Juantereno in the 1977 Central American and Caribbean Championships. I mean, honestly Tony, how did you do it?

In fact, my bowling run-up was pretty close to how I would approach my run-up to the pit when I was competing in the long jump. The timing of your run for the long jump has to be precise or you go nowhere. There is little room for error with that take-off point. It has to be a relaxed, rhythmical, light-on-your-feet approach to get the best result. Sound familiar? Long jump was also the reason I bowled so few no-balls because I knew exactly where my feet were going to land.

Inevitably, I started to play more cricket for school, initially for the school's Junior Colts team, which was for under-14s. I was captained by Sydney Headley, one of the sons of the legendary George Headley. Sydney was a very good cricketer, who specialised with the bat and was also a dangerous slow bowler. He was also a great thinker about the game, even at that young age. He could have made a fine cricketer, but he didn't persevere. Instead he moved to Africa to be closer to his roots and, in his words, 'do what he could for his people'. He was always that way inclined. He is still there.

The under-16 team was the next port of call, but I found I was playing more and more for Melbourne Cricket Club. Trevor Parchment, the school games master, had heard I was playing a lot for Melbourne and doing reasonably well, and thought I should be in the team that represented the school in the Sunlight Cup Competition. It was the major schoolboy competition in Jamaica.

I was invited down for practice and was picked for the team immediately, although I didn't think I was a popular selection with the captain. After all, it was something of a promotion. I got the impression that my selection was forced on him. In my first game his usual two new ball bowlers weren't very effective; two spinners then had a go without much success and then, finally, I was thrown the ball, with the opposition very few wickets down and looking fairly comfortable. I took two wickets in my first spell. The skipper realised I wasn't too bad. By 1970, at the age of 16, I was a regular in the KC Sunlight Cup team and in 1973, in my last year, I captained them to an unbeaten season. It was tremendous fun for me – and that's all I thought it would ever be. But cricket would suddenly start to become a bit more serious.

2

JAMAICA DAYS

The same year that I left Kingston College, but before the school year had ended, I made my first-class debut for my country, Jamaica. I was just 18. Just over two years later I had made my Test debut for West Indies against Australia. It was some progression for a guy whose goal at that stage of life was just to play sport as often as possible. And have as much fun as possible doing it!

Throughout my formative cricket years playing in the Rankine Cup, for Melbourne and Kingston College, I would just turn up and bowl. That was all I thought necessary to do myself justice, so I had no reason to change when I was performing well enough to be selected for Jamaica in the Caribbean Under-19s tournament for three successive years between 1971 and 1973. Each year the tournament would be held on a different island and every island in the region would send a team to compete.

The standard of cricket was high and many future West Indies cricketers got their first taste of territorial competition in those tournaments. In those three years I played against Colin Croft, Faoud Bacchus and Larry Gomes, who went on to play Test cricket for the West Indies, and many others who represented their respective countries at the senior level. Just turning up and bowling as quickly as I could proved to be enough to ensure I did well. However, the under-19 tournaments were not first-class cricket and having impressed enough to be picked to play for the full Jamaica team against Barbados on 19 January 1973, I discovered I had to bridge a gulf between the two levels.

When I turned up at Sabina Park for that first game, I found out what a fit fast bowler was – and it wasn't me. It came as a shock, I can tell you, because I thought I was in great condition. After all, I'd been playing the game for years.

Before the match I had seen Uton Dowe, a fast bowler who played four Tests for West Indies, running around on the outfield and coming back to the dressing room to get a skipping rope out. I thought he was mad. 'He'll be too tired to bowl,' I said to myself. It was called warming up.

Admittedly Dowe was the exception. In the early 1970s, teams arrived at the ground an hour before the game was due to start. Tracksuit was a word they did not have in their vocabulary. There were no nets to speak of. Batsmen would have a few throwdowns in their whites for ten minutes, usually in front of the pavilion, and then everyone would go back in and wait for the captain to inform them of the result of the toss. Of course, being new to the team I did exactly the same. We had our feet up when the skipper told us that we would be fielding.

I was given the new ball. After a couple of overs I was gone, dead on my feet. At my fielding position at fine leg I was holding onto the fence to prevent myself from falling over, panting, sweating and generally in a terrible state. I was hoping no one would notice. I was also hoping that by the time I had finished my fourth over, the captain would not ask me back for a fifth. But he did. I was so out of it I don't know how I got through the over. I can't remember a single ball that I bowled and I was just on autopilot, praying I would make it to the end without embarrassing myself.

The problem was that I had never been a big one for training. Until this point, no problem, I could rock up and bowl six or seven overs without puffing too hard. Straight off the reel. But this showed me how fit I needed to be for first-class cricket. I think nerves were to blame, too. Despite having no aspirations to play the game at the highest level, I was desperate to do well for myself. There were people in the stands who had come to see this talked-about fast bowler and I wanted to put on a good show. I tried to bowl too fast.

It was a shock to the system that I had to put right. I eventually started going to the gym, lifting weights and doing a lot of running. Fitness would be central to my success as a cricketer, but that came later under the tutelage of fitness coach Dennis Waight, who was appointed to the team for the Packer series. With Dennis's help, the West Indies team found out about the importance of being in the best possible condition. Dennis was only supposed to be our physiotherapist, but he was interested in our progress and became very close to the team as a whole. One day he went to Clive Lloyd and told him that he thought for a group of professional cricketers, we were nowhere near as fit as we should be. Clive gave him free reign and the rest is history. More about Dennis later, but we were the fittest team around and it was no coincidence we were the best team, too.

That first year I played only a few games for Jamaica. I was just getting my feet wet, becoming accustomed to the step up from Melbourne games and under-19 cricket. Despite my scarce appearances, I was selected to play in the President's XI against Australia in that same first-class debut year. It was a surprise because being picked for such a game often meant that a player was considered to be just a step away from the West Indies team. I reasoned that with the game being played in Jamaica, the West Indies Cricket Board was trying to save money on air fares, hence the reason for plumping for me.

Besides, there were bowlers like Vanburn Holder, Keith Boyce and Uton Dowe who were well ahead of me in the pecking order. Granted I had come to attention because I twice clean-bowled Australia batsman Ian Redpath in a game for Jamaica, but there was no way I was getting ahead of myself thinking I was Mr Big because I'd castled a Test batsman. I repeated the trick for a third time in four innings against Redpath for the President's XI, though. But apart from that, there weren't too many other wickets under the belt.

If playing for Jamaica was a learning curve, then the curve would have been in the shape of a smile. I seemed to spend most of my time laughing. Guys like Maurice Foster, Lawrence Rowe, Dowe, Leonard Levy, Sam Morgan, Renford Pinnock and Neville McKoy took me under their wing. They treated me like I was their younger brother.

All of them were great personalities, in particular Pinnock, who we called Pinny. He was a born joker. Once during a game when it started to rain, he walked on to the wicket and pretended to cover it by laying his handkerchief on the pitch and then disappearing to the pavilion. He had an answer to everything and could have us roaring with laughter in the most tense situation.

One of those was the final trial match played that year at Sabina Park for selection for a Jamaica side to play in the Shell Shield, the big domestic competition in the Caribbean. The selectors would watch the game from the pavilion and on the last day, having made up their minds, they would put the names of the chosen few on the scoreboard. The result was players not concentrating on the game, constantly straining their necks to look at the scoreboard rather than the ball. And if you were in the dressing room, you certainly weren't watching the action, instead nervously eyeing that board while chewing fingernails down to the bone.

The team I was on was batting and everyone was edgy. Enter Pinny, who pointed to the scoreboard and said sarcastically, 'If they don't give me a game, I'm not playin'.' With that one joke he relaxed us all as we fell about laughing.

I used to tell this story about Pinny, and many others, to my West Indies teammates when we were trying to kill time in hotel rooms around the world and as a result Pinny became revered by the guys.

When Malcolm Marshall met Pinny at a festival match that Melbourne Club would stage every year, he told him, 'I've heard so much about you, you're the man that's been making me laugh for years. You're the man that said, if they don't pick you, you weren't playing.'

Pinny shook his hand and replied, 'I tell you something Maco, with yourself, Garner, Croft and Roberts around ... if they give me a game now, I'm still not playing.' It was all tongue in cheek. Pinny was a good batsman and scored big runs against some of the best bowlers around, including the lethally quick Charlie Griffith and Wes Hall. It was unfortunate for him that he was around at a time when West Indies had so many good batsmen, otherwise he would have been a success at inter-national level, too.

Pinny was about 5ft 9in and stocky, often the stature for good batsmen. He always wore his cricket cap, whether off the field or on it, and he was a tremendous fidgeter at the crease – far worse than I was when I sat in those Sabina Park seats, pining to be elsewhere. He had a ritual before every ball. He would mark his crease, touch the top of his pads, then his box, the peak of his cap and finally adjust his shirt sleeves. Every time. The crowd in the stands loved him for it.

He took things slightly more seriously when batting, but in the field he thought he was a stand-up comic. When he was at fine leg for Jamaica in a game against the Australians, he appealed for a leg before when Greg Chappell was struck on the pads. He was the only fielder to do so because it was going a long way down the leg side. Chappell gave him a look as if he had lost his mind and even the umpire was a bit shocked. At the end of the over when Pinny was changing fielding positions, the umpire enquired, 'What are you doing, Pinny? You couldn't possibly see whether it was out from down there,' he said.

'That was why I appealed,' replied Pinny. 'I couldn't see whether it was out or not, so I had to ask.'

Pinny was not the only one with a quick wit. Leonard Levy, our offspinner and affectionately known as Uncle Sunny, could have us rolling around, too. In a Shield game in the Leeward Islands against what was then called the Combined Islands, he came up with a good one-liner. One late evening, approaching close of play, our captain, Maurice Foster, asked Uncle Sunny, who was number 11, to go in as nightwatchman in order to protect Lawrence Rowe. Rowe was our number three and not long before had debuted for West Indies with a double century and century against New Zealand. The explanation given to Uncle Sunny was that it was getting a bit dark and he didn't want to risk Rowe in poor light. Like a flash, Uncle Sunny quipped, 'But skipper, if the world's best batsman can't see it because it's too dark, how am I going to see it?' We all roared with laughter, even Maurice, but the job was still Uncle Sunny's. Thankfully we didn't lose a wicket and he wasn't required.

If things were going well on the pitch, it was more important that they were going well off it. I needed a career. In those days I couldn't earn a living through cricket alone in the Caribbean. The only way to make cricket a career was to sign a professional contract in England. Playing for West Indies was not lucrative, an observation that may raise a few eyebrows given the amounts players earn today. I remember a Test match against India in

Guyana in 1976 when we were being paid US$200 per Test. Not a ball was bowled because of rain and the money went down the drain with it. We didn't get a penny – no match, no pay.

When I became established as an international bowler, I was offered contracts to play county cricket by Sussex and Lancashire. The Sussex deal was put together by Tony Greig, the England captain, soon after I took 14 wickets against his team at The Oval in 1976. It was an attractive package: a sponsored car, a house for accommodation (in case people think I was getting the house for myself) and £10,000 a year, which in 1976 was an awful lot of money. Lancashire, too, wanted my signature and I would have been more inclined to go there because of skipper Clive Lloyd, but they didn't offer as much as Sussex.

Obviously Mr Greig saw something he liked at The Oval that day. Why did I turn these contracts down? Simply, I did not see myself as a professional cricketer. It had not been a goal of mine growing up because I had always been aware that it was hard to earn a living from the game in the Caribbean.

My mum, who was a schoolteacher, unsurprisingly made it clear that exams and qualifications were important. 'You need a piece of paper behind your name, Mikey,' she told me repeatedly.

At school I loved anything to do with numbers, mainly because I found words so tiresome. It was a bit of an escape, getting lost in all those calculations. My habit of fidgeting would return in those long, drawn-out history and English lessons.

With my love of calculations, it was fitting that my first job was in Barclays Bank in Kingston. They were just becoming computerised and I was assigned to the computer centre. I actually didn't last long, barely a year in fact. I needed time off work to play for Jamaica in 1974, which I had to apply for through the manager. I was allowed leave, but it was unpaid.

On my return from a game, the manager of the bank called me into his office and asked me, 'What are your intentions? We can't have you leaving all the time to go and play cricket.' He gave me an ultimatum – Barclays or cricket.

Rudi Cohen, who was a very good player for Jamaica, a fast bowler in fact, had been given the same choice by Barclays, but unlike me he had a very good job there and decided to give up the game. (He later migrated to the United States and still lives in Connecticut, where he has close connections to the cricket Hall of Fame movement there.) However, after the meeting at the bank, I went straight home and wrote my letter of resignation. I was still living with my parents at the time so there was not a pressing need for me to find work.

Michael Manley, author of the book *History of West Indies Cricket* and the fourth prime minister of Jamaica, heard that I was kicking my heels at home; by this time my name was well known and Manley was a huge cricket fan, so he organised an interview for me at the government's Central Data Processing Unit on East Street. In other words, computers. I went down there and got the job. Working in a government department meant mandatory time off if you were representing your country at sport – with pay, too. In addition I was being trained to be a computer programmer. It was fantastic. They were delighted for me to continue my cricket career. I had the best of both worlds and I still have many friends from my days working there. Loris Abrahams, a wonderful lady, was my boss and we are still in touch. I kept that job right up until 1981 when I got a contract to play for Rishton in the Lancashire League.

But I digress, I am getting ahead of myself. There was the small matter of selection for West Indies in 1975. It was the start of a magnificent time in my life. My timing could not have been better because, unlike few Caribbean cricketers before us, the team would be revered and handsomely rewarded.

3

PLAYING DAYS

When I said that the call from West Indies would be the beginning of a wonderful time for me, I should have used the word 'eventually' as a caveat. My first experience of international cricket left a bitter taste, and following my first tour to Australia in 1975–76, I considered whether my thirst for the big stage had been slaked.

I spat the dummy, that's for sure. I had such a miserable time on that trip that it would not have bothered me if I had never played again. I said as much to my father as my inexperienced and impetuous mind mulled over whether I should pack up.

My selection for West Indies had been a surprise to a lot of people. I had only played a handful of first-class games and had only taken one five-wicket haul during that time; unsurprisingly a few eyebrows were raised. I was no immediate success, no tyro fast bowler who burst on to the scene, blasting batsman's stumps to all parts of the Caribbean. No. I was a bowler who supposedly had potential and that was why I was selected. Clive Lloyd was made West Indies captain in 1974 and he saw something that he liked when I played for Jamaica against his team, Guyana.

Guyana's Bourda ground had a reputation as a graveyard for fast bowlers, with Roy Fredericks, Len Baichan, Alvin Kallicharran and Lloyd the men ready to do the digging. This intimidating line-up and others before their time, which included players like Rohan Kanhai, Joe Solomon and Basil Butcher, had buried many a bowler, including the extremely quick Roy Gilchrist from my native Jamaica, thanks to their skill and the easy-paced nature of the pitch. Indeed, I had suffered at Guyana's hands the previous year on a much more bowler-friendly pitch in Jamaica at Sabina Park. For 24 overs I toiled and sweated to no avail as Lloyd (I'm sure I had him leg before at least once in three huge appeals!) and Kallicharran both notched centuries.

So I knew what could be in store. However, I was confident this time around that perhaps I could do some damage. I was a different bowler, had gotten a bit more experience and was a touch stronger. My run-up was smoother and more rhythmical and I had added a yard of pace, thanks to some conditioning work and increasing my stamina.

By now I was taking the new ball for Jamaica and in my first spell I removed Fredericks for eight and Kallicharran for a duck. I came back later to get another couple of wickets to help Jamaica to first-innings points. Well, I knew on that wicket and against those batsmen I had made a statement. Lloyd agreed and I guess that he had remembered how I bowled a year previously, noted my improvement and reckoned that if I continued such an advance, I could be of use to him and West Indies.

I had a bit of a hint that I could be selected for the tour to Australia because when the selectors met to pick a World Cup squad to go to England in 1975, I had been discussed. J K Holt Jnr, a former Jamaica and West Indies batsman and at that time a selector, knew my father and told him that my name had come up. Lloyd said that he didn't want me to be selected because a one-day tour was no launching pad for a young bowler. How times have changed.

I can remember exactly where I was when I found out about

my selection for the 1975–76 tour of Australia. Those days, there was no personal call from either selectors or representative of the board – you heard through the press or an announcement on the radio. I was at my club, Melbourne, with touring a long way from my mind when the news came through.

When I was given the nod I can't say the feeling was one of elation. Australia was an awfully long way away and instead of my first thoughts being what it would be like to take a Test wicket, the only thing that occupied my mind was 'I'm going to be away for Christmas'. I had always thought – still do – that Christmas is a time for family and I looked forward to it tremendously. This was going to be my first Christmas away from home and family.

Having never really dreamt of playing for West Indies, to say I was overwhelmed would be an overstatement. I would watch the matches, listen to the commentary on the radio and hear the chatter about all these great players, but my love was just playing the game.

There was no big celebration at the Holding household either when I was picked for West Indies. Sure, my parents were proud and they were big cricket fans, regularly attending Sabina Park, but they never made me think that I was now suddenly better than anyone else just because I had been given that famous maroon cap. There was no formal recognition, not even a handshake I don't think, and certainly no cocktail party, nothing like that. Just congratulations. My parents were never ones to get too carried away by anything, at least not in my presence.

Looking back, that understated approach was fitting, given the grim time I had in Australia. On that tour, everything that could go wrong did go wrong.

We were well beaten (5–1 in a six-Test series), there was squabbling among the players and when I got back from that tour, which also saw some, shall we say, unconventional umpiring, I said to my father, 'If this is West Indies cricket or Test cricket, you can forget it. I don't want to be a part of it.'

Coping with defeat is a part of sport, and while I obviously found it difficult, the most upsetting aspect of the tour was the infighting.

It was fractious as soon as we set foot on Australian soil and as a young player I just could not understand why so many players seemed intent on causing trouble. We were tearing ourselves apart and it had a huge bearing on the result. It was a massive culture shock for me because the Jamaica dressing room was always a happy place, full of laughter and jokes, even when we didn't do too well. And believe me, we didn't win too many games away from home in those early days.

A poisonous atmosphere surrounding a team can be very damaging for young players. We had a lot of experience in the team with players like Lloyd, Gibbs, Deryck Murray, Vanburn Holder and Keith Boyce, but also several cricketers on either their first or second tours. A long way from home, they needed an arm round the shoulder and a harmonious group. Having experienced the opposite, I can see why so many young players have gone on their first tour and never recovered, especially if they have performed with mediocrity.

Surprisingly, part of the problem was Clive Lloyd. He was an inexperienced captain on that tour and reckoned that as professionals we should all know what needed to be done to make sure we were fully prepared. The common statement from him was, 'You're all big men.' He left it up to us. The management left it up to us. That was a mistake because players so often try to get away with as much as possible. Give them an inch and they'll take a mile.

I found this attitude appalling from my teammates, particularly when they showed no respect to Lloyd and the team manager, Esmond Kentish, a former Jamaica fast bowler and friend of my father, with the way they spoke to them at various times. One player went as far as to tell the captain, when he found out that he was not in the final XI, that he didn't intend to be 12th man either.

Rows would start and occasionally boil over. It was more than a clash of personalities, that's for sure. One such incident when things got too heated was a team meeting at the Windsor Hotel in Melbourne. Alvin Kallicharran and Keith Boyce became embroiled in an argument about the hook shot, which had cost us quite a few wickets. It resulted in Kallicharran storming out of the team meeting. The management just let him go. There was no attempt to call him back or say, 'Hey, you've said your piece, now let's work through it.' I had never seen anything like it. Up until that point, as one of the junior squad members, I had kept my head down, but I could not let this pass. I ran after Kallicharran to try to get him to come back but he was not having any of it.

Australia had won the first Test at Brisbane by eight wickets and I made my debut with my father watching from the stands. I shared the new ball with Andy Roberts for the first time, but I would end up wicketless. In fact, I made more of an impact with the bat. In the first innings, I made 34 in an innings described by *Wisden* as 'bold'. So impressed was my captain that I was promoted immediately to nightwatchman in the second innings, hanging around for almost an hour.

My first Test wicket came at Perth at the WACA, which at the time and for many years after, was like Mecca for fast bowlers because of the lightning quick wicket and steep carry. The first of four wickets for me in Australia's first innings was Max Walker. As time has flown by, I keep thinking that people not too knowledgeable about cricketing history will think he was a top batsman, but with so much information so readily available these days, I think I'm living in hope. Ian Chappell was numbered among the other three though, and he was no mug, never mind that he had 156 runs already under his belt. Andy Roberts was the star though, as we won the match by an innings and 87 runs. He took seven for 54 in the second innings, the top seven in the order, leaving Bernard Julien to get rid of the bowlers, Walker, Lillee and Thomson.

Sadly, this game would prove to be the high point of the whole trip and our morale seemed to dip with each day of cricket we played. One of the main reasons for the tension and irritation was the umpiring. It set the already unstable camp on edge because we felt it was in favour of the home side. Hang on, I've been too kind there. We were sure it was in favour of the home side.

For me it all came to a head in Sydney, the venue of the fourth Test. After the comprehensive victory in Perth, we lost in Melbourne, but we had an outstanding chance of levelling the series after making 355 in the first innings, and when Australia batted they were going along nicely until they lost two wickets in quick succession. The second of those was my old friend Ian Redpath, who I had caught behind by Deryck Murray first ball after tea. From my second ball after the break, I had another catch at the wicket. At least I thought I did.

Ian Chappell had come to the wicket to replace Redpath and at 93–2 we had the Australians in some bother. We knew that if we could get Ian out cheaply, we would be in with a real victory chance because we rated him as their best batsman and most prized scalp.

I was trying to bowl him an inswinger, hoping his feet would be a little slow having just come in, but having delivered from wide of the crease it moved away from him on pitching. Another one of those deliveries that I can't fully take credit for. Chappell drove loosely at it and got a chunky edge that flew safely and snugly into Murray's gloves. The appeal was unanimous. It felt almost a waste of breath because the edge was so thick. But umpire Reg Ledwidge was not moving. Chappell wasn't either. Well, he was, but only to turn his back and mark his guard with that trademark style of his with the sprigs in his shoe. All Ledwidge did was shake his head with a silly smirk on his face. I totally lost it. I wandered out towards the covers and sunk to my haunches.

I am not ashamed to say that I began to weep. We were fighting back in a series that had been lopsided because of the at best, incompetent, or at worst, biased, umpiring, fighting to become a recognised team and fighting among ourselves. It all became too much for me and the tears began to flow.

It felt as though my heart had been ripped out. Sure, I was a grown man and getting the sniffles was probably not the best way to react, but I felt as though I had gone back in time to my childhood, playing Catchy Shubby on the scrubland behind Dunrobin Avenue with kids refusing to hand over the bat when it was clear they were out.

This was Test cricket. This was not supposed to happen. This was the highest level of the game, millions were watching on television, records were being kept and I had been denied a wicket when the whole ground had seen Chappell hit the ball into Murray's gloves. Chappell later stated it was the most embarrassing moment in his career, but he was just not a walker, it's not the way he played.

Lance Gibbs had spotted that I was in a bad way and came over to comfort me. I told him that I would not bowl another ball. Of course, I did and I soon had Chappell caught behind for four. Same delivery, same shot, but this time a different response from the umpire.

Ironically, it was his brother, Greg, who would take the game away from us with an unbeaten 182 in that innings, but not before being dropped in the slip cordon fairly early in his innings. This incident caused more antagonism as well. Clive Lloyd had been contracted by a local paper in Australia to do some columns during the series and he commented on the dropped catch in his article. He innocently implied that if that catch had been taken, perhaps the end result of the Test could have been different. Well, the gentleman responsible for dropping the catch didn't take kindly to the inference and made it well known that he was unhappy with the comment. It seemed an innocent remark, but that's what happens when teams have no camaraderie and things are out of control. In those days of no internet or mobile phones, I wrote a letter back home telling everyone that although the series score stood at 3–1 at that point, it would be 5–1 by the end. I saw what was coming.

I was delighted to get back to Jamaica after the tour. There was still a sense of bewilderment and anger, though. My inexperienced and naïve mind couldn't comprehend what had gone on. We were sitting around the dinner table when I made the comment that I wasn't bothered about carrying on. I had missed the family Christmas, had a miserable time thanks to some unprofessional teammates and umpires, and was paid about EC$1,700 for the tour. I was still living at home at the time, but with about 2.7 Eastern Caribbean dollars to the US dollar, it was not the sort of wage that would encourage you to carry on. I wasn't enjoying myself and I wasn't earning money. What was the point?

Mum and Dad didn't really react. They knew that this was the impetuosity of youth talking. Dad was a real cool cucumber – unless he was at his job as a contractor when he could be quite vociferous and use language that would make your ears go red – and just advised me to cool off. He didn't say, 'No, you can't do that.' He knew that when I had calmed down and thought things through, I would continue playing.

My parents were very proud that I played for West Indies, but they would never really let me know how they felt. And they would never have said to me, 'You've got to carry on so I can walk around and be proud of my son.' Nothing like that, ever. If I stopped playing there was no way one of them would say, 'Hey, what are you doing?' Besides, cricket was not something which, if you gave it up, would be deemed as a stupid career decision. As I've said, you couldn't make a living from it in the Caribbean, and Mum had always wanted me to go to university to get a degree, or 'that piece of paper' as she called it, because she never thought cricket was more than a sport, definitely not a career.

At no time did I make my negative feelings public. Saying something like that over the dinner table is one thing, in the press or on the radio something else entirely. And those days, you weren't hounded by the press for quotes and opinions as cricketers are now. Talk was cheap, I suppose, because if it came to the crunch, I doubt whether I could really have said 'no' to the selectors. I loved playing cricket, I had no responsibilities living with my parents, so why not keep playing?

Thankfully, things did change. Clive Lloyd changed his management style. A captain those days was more than just the person who managed things on the field of play, and as I have stated so many times, he became a father figure to us all and a great captain. In my time the West Indies dressing room was never as acrimonious again (although there were problems on my final tour in New Zealand in 1987), and I was able to build good and lasting friendships. I did the same with members of the opposition too, although not quite to the same degree.

Perhaps if the New Zealand tour of 1980 had followed straight after that first trip Down Under, I definitely would have packed up and looked elsewhere. That tour will, of course, forever be remembered as infamous and it was another case of

'The Umpire Strikes Back'. Instead we had a home tour against India and then I went on tour to England. I wouldn't need the umpires there.

4

FIRST TRIP TO ENGLAND

I had never been to England before. I arrived on a chilly and damp May morning in 1976. I had heard plenty about what sort of place it was through friends and my mum, who lived there when she was studying to become a teacher. Cold. That was what most of them said, although Mum loved her time in what she called 'the mother country'.

They were right. I expected the sort of weather we got in those first few weeks, but that didn't mean that I had to like it. In fact, I'm not too sure whether I have ever really recovered from those frosty starts because these days I avoid cold weather at all costs, timing my arrival back at my Newmarket home from my winter retreats in Miami and the Caribbean to coincide with the English summer, or at least the months described as summer.

It was a culture shock that I initially struggled with on that first tour. The damp conditions underfoot caused problems in my delivery stride and then I caught a mystery bug (I blame the drop in temperature hampering my body's natural defences!). It took me a long time to recover and lots of convincing from my bowling partner, Andy Roberts, that even if the sun was shining brightly, it wasn't necessarily warm outside. When the heat did finally accompany the sun – and we went on to have the driest and hottest summer of the century – I had a hot streak of my own. I don't think it was a coincidence.

I took 28 wickets in four Tests at an average of 12. At The Oval, venue for the fifth Test, I took 14 wickets in the match. Nine of those were bowled as I made sure that I couldn't be denied by any funny umpiring, although in truth that was never likely to happen in England because the officials there were extremely competent and less prone to 'home town' decisions.

Before the series began I was still an unknown quantity. A bowler of potential. After the series, I don't think it would be too cocky to suggest that I was beginning to realise some of that promise. People had not heard much about me previously and it made me feel good that I had succeeded and made a name for myself. After my mediocre returns of 10 wickets in five Tests in Australia, the successes of the India series at home and now against England in England were heartwarming. Leaving England that summer, my emotions were in stark contrast to how I had felt the last time I had returned to the Caribbean following the Australian tour, which had left me feeling down and contemplating my cricketing future.

But we were back in action quickly after Australia. The series we hosted against India would shape the make-up of our team for the next twenty-odd years and change the face of international cricket forever. Lance Gibbs, the last great West Indies spinner, had played his final Test in 1976 in Melbourne, and Clive Lloyd, who in tandem with manager Clyde Walcott, was now getting the correct level of respect from players, was not convinced of the quality of his replacements. Raphick Jumadeen, a slow left-armer, the off spinner Albert Padmore and leg spinners David Holford and Imtiaz Ali had failed to make an impression in two Tests at the Queen's Park Oval in Trinidad. One of those Tests we lost, which enabled India to level the series after we had won the first Test comfortably in Barbados. We had set India 403 runs in the last innings to win the Test with three spinners in our team. Surely on a wearing Queen's

Park pitch, where spinners were supposed to rule the roost, they had no chance? Not so: India won comfortably with the spinners failing to make an impact.

As a result we went into the final Test of the series at Sabina Park, Jamaica, needing to win with the series tied at 1–1. Clive decided that he would go in with four fast bowlers. If the philosophy of relying on pure pace had begun to take root in Australia, it blossomed against India. On a fast, not to mention controversial, pitch at Sabina Park, we won under considerable public pressure. Clive would never rely on spin again.

That series was only my second, but with Andy Roberts resting an ankle injury, I was the spearhead of the attack. That gave me great confidence and I did quite well, taking 19 wickets.

I still had a lot to learn, though. That much was evident soon after arriving in England, when I played in an early tour match against Hampshire and struggled because of the damp run-ups and green landing areas inside the batting crease. It had never crossed my mind that I would need different bowling boots for different surfaces. I was trying to bowl with fixed studs, which were perfectly adequate on the harder pitches of the Caribbean or Australia, and would have been fine if they were new and as long as they were when the boots were first bought.

In early May in England they were not so good. I was struggling to get proper traction. Every time my front foot went down it would slip because there was quite a lot of grass around the batting crease. (Back then groundsmen did not bother to shave that area of grass.) I managed four wickets in the match but Vanburn Holder took five wickets in an innings with a far more controlled display. I was very unhappy on the bus back to the hotel after the match; I sat on my own with my face on the floor so to speak.

Clyde Walcott spotted that I was down and came to sit beside me. He asked what the problem was. I said to him that I had only one pair of boots and they were obviously the wrong sort for me to bowl in England as I was struggling with my footing. He told me to have a chat with Andy Roberts. 'He's been playing here for years,' Clyde said. 'Ask him where he gets his boots from.'

Andy soon put me in touch with a company in Northampton where I managed to buy some boots with screw-in studs that could be replaced every time they wore down, rather than the fixed ones. I was happy for the rest of the tour because I had boots for all conditions. And by the way, what you read above is correct: 'buy' is the applicable verb. This was long before the phenomenon of lots of free gear from manufacturers. Maybe the batsmen got their stuff free, but not us bowlers.

I was grateful for Clyde's intervention. A lot of people think he was a bit sarcastic at times, the way he dealt with people. I found him a good man manager, though. I was still a junior member of the side, he didn't need to take time to sit with me, but he tried to make sure everyone in the camp who he was responsible for was happy.

Next up against MCC I took seven wickets in the match at Lord's – inspired by my first appearance on the famous ground – and I was beginning to find my feet.

Alas, that darn cold had got into my bones, at least that's my story and I'm sticking to it. In the first weeks of the tour I was struck down with what the doctors reckoned was glandular fever. They said my tour was over and advised the management team that they should make plans to send me home. Supposedly, even after getting over the initial weakness and leaving the hospital, I would not have had enough recovery time to take part in the rest of the tour. Glandular fever usually took months to get over completely.

Thankfully I managed to talk the management round. I told them I would be fine in a few days, which was something of a gamble because I was in hospital and feeling very weak. My neck was badly swollen and I was so lethargic that I could barely get up to change the channel on the television (there was no remote control around in those days!) or go to the bathroom. It was depressing but luckily the doctor's prognosis was overly pessimistic. It can't have been glandular fever because I actually recovered rather quickly. More likely it was a bad case of mumps.

I missed the first Test at Nottingham, but was back for the second at Lord's, although if the truth be told, I was still not yet 100 per cent ready. I had to do a fitness test before the toss to convince Lloydie and the manager that I was fit enough. That consisted of me running in and bowling at top pace in the nets for a few overs and although I seemed to be at good pace, I was totally knackered at the end. I was hoping we would win the toss and bat to give me some more time but as luck would have it, we were in the field first. Viv Richards missed that Test as he was the next man to go down sick that tour. I was rooming with him at the time and unfortunately I must have managed to pass whatever I had on to him so he didn't play at Head-quarters. Viv broke the record for most calendar runs that year and no doubt had I not given him the dreaded lurgy, he would have scored even more runs. Sorry about that, Viv!

He had scored 556 runs in six innings against India and despite the setback I caused him, his brilliance reached new levels with 829 runs in his four Tests in England. We were both in rude health at The Oval. He got 291 and I got my 14 wickets.

People often tell me that they can't understand how I took wickets on that Oval pitch because it was flat, dry and hard, with the ball unable to bounce over waist height. I tell them it was all down to youthful enthusiasm and the sun warming my back. At 22 years of age, I had no fear and perhaps where the more mature bowlers reckoned the way to approach such a surface was to conserve energy and hit line and length, I absolutely tore in. My rhythm was good, and I felt strong and fit having completely got over my illness.

Once you get such a combination of rhythm and fitness when you're a young bowler, you just want to keep on running in and bowling fast. Wickets falling don't do any harm either. My first wicket of the 14 was Bob Woolmer from the Pavilion End. I told Clive Lloyd that I wanted to switch ends and the remaining 13 wickets came from the Vauxhall End. Everything just clicked.

One incident in that Test really stands out and I have never forgotten it. I mention it to prove how your mind can run away with you and how you feel that you are the centre of attention when you are doing well. In that first innings on my way to figures of eight for 92 – the best analysis of my career – I was on a hat-trick and England were nine wickets down. My mind was on the hat-trick ball because I had never claimed one before. Lloyd called a quick team conference before the last batsman came to the wicket and I thought that he must be planning the best way for me to claim the feat, demanding all the fielders were on their toes so the young Holding could be the hero.

I approached the huddle feeling ten feet tall and with a bit of a swagger. I was totally surprised and slightly perturbed to discover Lloyd was not discussing me at all, instead talking about enforcing the follow-on. He wanted to know what the team thought about batting again.

It was an important moment in my career. It made me realise that it wasn't all about me. It was about West Indies and the West Indies team. Little things like that are a huge help. Sometimes you see some people playing and you know just by watching them that they reckon it's all about them and not the country they play for. I was so pleased that I was made aware of the importance of the team at an early stage.

The wickets that stick in my memory from that Test are Tony Greig's, without a shadow of a doubt. They were two fast yorkers – one was actually more of a full toss – and they sent his stumps flying. The greatest sight for a fast bowler.

Greig had made himself a target. His ill-judged comments at the start of the series that he would make us 'grovel' riled us to the extent that we needed no further motivation. It was an extremely insensitive remark to make about a largely black team. Remember he was a white South African, qualified for England only via his parents, and to make such a statement sent the wrong message, pure and simple. We saw nothing else.

Every time he came to the crease the fast bowlers found an extra yard of pace. There was a great sense of joy when we got him out in that series. 'You're going to make us grovel? No, you won't.' Greig committed the cardinal sin in cricket, or any sport come to think of it. He made things personal whether he meant to or not. But that is Tony Greig. As far as I'm concerned, he got as far as he did in the game not just on pure ability, but because he was such a competitor. He was a decent player but he recognised that when you're not the most talented in the world, you need that little bit extra. He wanted to outsmart the opposition, mentally and tactically. His intentions were to play on our minds and make us think 'this guy's going to try to get on top of us'.

Greig could not have got it more wrong. It was almost as if he was saying we had no backbone and painted the Caribbean people as fair-weather cricketers. Everything was fine in our team until it got rough. Then it falls apart. That was what he was saying.

Undoubtedly he was wrong. Undoubtedly it backfired.

There is no ill-feeling towards Greig now, nor from the people of the Caribbean. It is water under the bridge and I've spent a lot of time with Greigy since then, doing commentary all around the world and I've got to know him well. You realise he was only trying to get a psychological edge over his opponents. In fact, Greig is hugely popular in the Caribbean. They love his commentary and his enthusiasm for the game. Besides, many times over, West Indies cricket has shown the world how we are capable of making the opposition grovel.

We certainly did that to Greig and his team. By the Oval Test we had already won the series, leading 2–0 with two draws in a five-Test series. I felt great that I was taking all these wickets because I needed to become a consistently good fast bowler. Australia had been disaster, although I bowled fast and that was recognised, I did well versus India and in England I needed to continue that progress.

On that tour up until The Oval, I'd taken 14 wickets in three Tests – that was no great shakes. So, with what would remain my fastest spell of bowling over a consistent period, I finally showed people that I belonged. It was a watershed moment.

5

THE PACKER YEARS

In 1976 I went back to school. Hardly fitting reward for someone who had just enjoyed a successful tour of England, you may think. But burying my nose in the textbooks had to be done. As I have said, you could not make a living out of cricket at that time, so instead of using brawn with ball in hand, it was time to engage the brain with the pen.

On my return to Jamaica after the tour, the then Jamaican prime minister, Michael Manley, offered me a scholarship to the University of the West Indies to study computer science. The term started in September so it must have been barely two weeks from leaving the field at The Oval to walking into the classroom again. I would not be there long, though. Around March 1977 I received a telephone call that would immediately change my life forever and set me on a learning curve about life that was steep and rapid.

The man on the other end of the line was Clive Lloyd, my West Indies captain, who at the time was leading the team against Pakistan in Trinidad. I was injured with a torn rotary muscle in my right shoulder, the result of all that effort I put in at The Oval. He told me that a man named Kerry Packer had contacted him to help set up something termed 'private enterprise cricket'. Well, I had never heard of Packer and I wasn't entirely sure what Clive meant by 'private enterprise'. He explained that Packer was a businessman and he wanted to stage a series between Australia and a World team.

The only questions I had for Clive, despite me being totally unaware of why the venture was being undertaken, was how it was being financed and by who, and whether he was going to play in it. Clive told me he was. I revered, respected and trusted Clive so that was good enough for me. Clive also told me that Andy Roberts had agreed to play and Viv Richards was mulling it over. Those three and myself were the four West Indians that Packer wanted in this World XI. He suggested I think on it and told me that Tony Greig, the England captain, and a Western Australian businessman called Austin Robertson, would be paying me a visit to go into more detail.

Well, I could have dropped the receiver. 'Tony Greig,' I blustered. 'Surely we don't want anything to do with him after what he said about us!' The 'grovel' remark still rankled with me and I was far from keen on him as a person. But Clive told me not to worry and advised me to 'just listen to what he has to say'. As usual, I took Clive's word.

Greig, of course, was taking a huge risk acting as a sort of secret player's agent for Packer and when World Series Cricket was announced, his standing in the game fell alarmingly, and he lost the captaincy of England. He was virtually ostracised by the establishment. He came to Jamaica and I met him and Robertson at the Sheraton Hotel. They showed me some magazine articles about Packer, plenty of paperwork proving how much he was worth and told me the television station he owned, Channel 9, would cover the matches live.

Packer had wanted to buy the broadcast rights for Australia's home Test matches as part of his plan to boost Channel 9's ailing ratings with top-class sports programming. He approached the Australia Cricket Board with $1.5 million – an offer that was reported to be eight times the size of the previous contract, but he lost out to the ABC, who had been broadcasting matches for 20 years. ABC paid only slightly more than $200,000 for three years.

When Packer was rebuffed by England's Test and County Cricket Board for an offer to broadcast the Australia tour of England in 1977 in favour of, you guessed it, ABC, he was so irked by what he was quoted as calling 'an old boy network' that he decided to set up World Series Cricket. Of course this was information I later gleaned; I knew nothing about all this when Greig and Robertson visited me.

Although Greig and Robertson were doing a fine job of explaining everything to me, I must admit it was all going over my head a bit. I wasn't really paying too much attention, mainly because I'd already decided that if Clive was going, so was I. It was as simple as that.

The mind focused that bit more, however, when it was revealed to me how much I would be paid. The amount of money Packer was offering was a far cry from what I had just finished earning playing against India in 1976 or even going to England for an entire summer. I earned US$200 per Test in the Caribbean; Packer was offering AUS$25,000 per year for a three-year contract. In those days, Australian dollars were worth more than US, so it was an incredible package.

There were two sticking points for me, though. First were the number of South Africans on the list of recruited players, which I was not happy about. I could not possibly play alongside cricketers whose country had inflicted apartheid on its people. I had long held strong views about the political situation there and if I was seen playing with these guys then people would reckon that I was somehow in favour of the regime or that the money had made me compromise my principles. I knew that Michael Manley was also anti-apartheid because he had supported the Gleneagles agreement, which had been drawn up by the Commonwealth countries that same year to discourage contact and competition between their sportsmen and sporting organisations and teams or individuals from South Africa. I was suddenly very doubtful.

I told Greig that I could not commit myself to the project until they had cleared it with Manley. If he didn't give me permission to play or be involved with South Africans in this way, I wouldn't go. They allowed me to sign on the dotted line with the proviso that Mr Manley had to clear the way first.

Apparently Packer himself called Manley. They came to an agreement that only South Africans who had played county cricket in England would be engaged. I believe it meant that Graeme Pollock, who may well be remembered as South Africa's greatest player, along with a few others, missed out as a result. And Packer missed out on a player who would have tempted many supporters along to the matches or to watch on television. Those who had already signed up were still paid the fees promised to them – they just couldn't take part.

With that compromise in place I was cleared to play, although there was still snag number two: I just didn't believe the whole thing would take place. I told Mum and Dad 'this seems too good to be true'. You have to remember that I had grown up knowing there was never any money in the game and now all of a sudden this Australian guy I'd never heard of was offering me the chance to make a living from it. Plus, there was no talk about this World Series, either among the press men or on the grapevine. Nothing. Usually, there is always someone who gets wind of such a story and I reasoned that the silence was because it was either rubbish or it had all fallen through. Greig had told me that I would receive a third of my fee before I had even bowled a ball. 'Thank you very much,' I said to him while I was thinking, 'I'll believe it when I see it.'

Two weeks after that meeting I took my savings book down

to the local Barclays branch to see whether I would be converted to believer status. I handed the book to the clerk, asking it to be updated. She put it in her machine, pressed a few buttons and handed it back. No money. I was sure the whole Packer thing was a joke.

I waited another week. I went back to Barclays, handed over the book, the clerk pressed some buttons and gave it back. For the first time in my life in that little blue account book I saw a comma. World Series Cricket was on.

My earnings from World Series Cricket allowed me to buy my first car. It was a white Mitsubishi Gallant, a former rental car. In Jamaica in the late 1970s, new cars weren't easily access-ible, but the second-hand vehicle was good enough as my first buy anyway. I'll never forget it. I drove around Jamaica thinking I was the swishiest thing on four wheels, which must have been a first for any owner of a Gallant and a second-hand one at that. Later I bought a house with my Packer earnings, a huge step forward for someone who was in his mid-twenties, although I had to get my sister Marjorie to act as guarantor for the mortgage.

The silence surrounding the planning of the World Series and the negotiations with players was exploded in May when some Australian journalists finally got hold of the story. The cricket world was rocking from this 'Packer Circus', as the media termed it, and immediately the Australian and English cricket boards, who believed they were directly threatened, went to war with the ringmaster. By talking about banning players – 13 of the 17 members of the Australia squad who were touring England at the time had signed – they picked a fight with the wrong man.

Packer, instead of folding, like the cricket boards hoped he would, was galvanised. It was a mark of the man and completely in character given how he had reacted when first denied broadcast rights. Perhaps others in his situation might have compromised their ambition. Not Packer. He expanded his horizons. He signed up the entire West Indies team to compete against his Australian team, plus others for a Rest of the World XI and another side, which was to be called the Cavalier XI. The cricket administrators then decided to ban all the Packer players from taking part in county cricket. Again Packer didn't take it lying down. He took them to court claiming restraint of trade and of course won the case when Justice Slade ruled against the ban on the players earning their living in county cricket.

There were 16 West Indians, 11 of who had toured England in 1976. Viv Richards had eventually decided to join the party and the only notable absentees were Alvin Kallicharran, Colin Croft and Vanburn Holder. Kallicharran had a contract to play county cricket for Warwickshire and they vetoed his involvement, while Croft would come for year two. Holder, I feel, was unlucky not to have been asked to join.

The 'player roster', if you will, today reads like a roll call of some cricket legends. For Australia there were the Chappell brothers, Dennis Lillee, Doug Walters and Rod Marsh. The Rest of the World boasted Greig, Alan Knott, John Snow, Dennis Amiss, Derek Underwood and Bob Woolmer from England, Zaheer Abbas, Majid Khan, Asif Iqbal and Imran Khan from Pakistan, while Eddie Barlow, Barry Richards and Mike Procter were some of the South Africans from the county circuit who were allowed to play.

Naively, I was taken by surprise by the rumpus. I was wet behind the ears in believing that it would not impact on West Indies cricket. As far as I was aware, the World Series schedule did not clash with any planned series and Packer had assured us that our careers would not be jeopardised. We would always be made available to represent our traditional West Indies team.

What else could I have asked for? I had accepted the scholarship to go to university because I never saw myself making a living from cricket, and now I was being offered the opportunity to play the game that I loved for proper reward and still remain available to my country.

Despite the West Indies Cricket Board not being affected, inevitably they were put under pressure by the other international boards and when we left for the first World Series event in the winter of 1977, we knew that it might tell at a later stage.

Some of the cat calls that were ringing in our ears were 'mercenary' and 'rebel'. My conscience was always clear, however, thank you very much. I was still available to play for West Indies so what exactly had I done wrong? Nothing, except for probably being a bit selfish in thinking only of myself and West Indies cricket. Packer was trying to change the game for the better and that included paying cricketers closer to what we were worth, although it must be said that at the time I thought I was being overpaid.

The fiercest critics, it seemed to me, were talking with their mouths full of sour grapes. They were former players, or ones coming to the end of their careers, who were jealous that they were not involved. In fact, I knew of some who were quite strident in their condemnation, but as soon as they were asked to be involved in the organisation, either in administration or commentary work, they jumped at it. So much for being upright and holy, as they claimed.

The first year of World Series was hard work and at times deflating. We weren't allowed to use the main cricket grounds and the stands were empty more times than not. Still, Packer made us know that if the project failed it would not be for want of money. We as cricketers had to do our part and he would do his, which was to supply all the finances needed. To emphasise how serious he was about the standard of cricket he was expecting, he gave the West Indies team an earful after one pretty ordinary performance. We had just played against Australia and were well beaten. Packer was not happy. This was not Packer the Australian fan who had just seen his team give the West Indies a proper hiding, this was Packer the businessman. He stormed into our dressing room at the end of the game and tore into us, using language that I can't repeat here. He let us know that the performance he had just witnessed was nowhere near the level he knew we were capable of. He left no one in any doubt that he was the paymaster and if we didn't perform we would be out. If any player had been going easy before that, thinking it was a joyride, they sure bucked up their ideas.

That incident showed how hard-nosed Packer could be. He was a businessman first and foremost, and the fact that it was his country that had beaten us did not matter. He was desperate for World Series to be a success and he knew that it wouldn't be if it was seen as 'soft'.

There was a lot of speculation in the press about how hard players would be trying in World Series; some even went as far as to suggest the matches were fixed. It was nonsense, of course. They were just trying to discredit the competition. Unfortunately, in its first year a lot of people believed the ballyhoo. Attendances were not as good as they could have been and it was obvious that Packer was struggling to stem a wave of adverse feeling started by the media. There were stories that Packer was seen counting the number of cars in the car park and during one match, a picture was taken of the West Indies players watching on television the action from an official Test played between India and Australia. The press lapped it up, printing the picture with the caption 'Even Packer's West Indians prefer real cricket'.

The negative press didn't stop after World Series Cricket ended, either. Some of the press were still after Packer. When his television station Channel 9 took over the broadcasts, it thought Packer had too much say in Australia's cricket. During the Australian summer of 1979–80, the very next summer after he pulled the plug on WSC, two teams instead of the usual one toured England and the West Indies. West Indies were there for a Test series and England came to take part in a triangular one-day international series afterwards. The last qualifying game had West Indies playing against Australia in Sydney and if West Indies won the game, the finals would be between us and England, with Australia out. Well, Australia went on to win a very close game with the help of some rain and one newspaper carried a story with the headline, 'Come on dollar, come on', which was a take-off of the catchy promotional song of the times, 'Come on Aussie, come on'. The article implied that West Indies had thrown the game to make sure that Australia made it to the finals. The inference was that we might have been influenced to do as such because of our Packer loyalties, resulting in better television ratings for Channel 9 and more interest from Australian crowds if Australia were in the finals. Needless to say, the newspaper carrying the article ended up in court, and Clive Lloyd, the captain, and the entire West Indies team that took part was awarded damages. Talk about easy? Well that was, but not the cricket we played during World Series Cricket.

In my opinion, World Series was tougher than the Tests being played at the time because we had all the best players. Laughably, some cricket journalists wrote that Australia were actually stronger without the Chappells, Marsh and Lillee. Incredible. Every game we played was hard when playing some of the best cricketers there had ever been. Indeed, even if we were playing in one of the warm-ups, you could get your head knocked off by one of the fastest bowlers in the world.

The schedule was continuous and a lot of travelling was involved, but this was not a huge bind because it was great to get around and see Australia. The Australia Cricket Board had banned Packer from using its cricket grounds so we would tour the country. We played in the big cities, but also the small country towns like Toowoomba, Rockhampton and Bendigo, to name but a few.

Mostly we were playing on football grounds and in Perth we played inside the trotting track at Gloucester Park. In Melbourne we had to play at VFL Park, which held 80,000, but there were only a few hundred in the ground – it was a surreal experience hearing the sound of leather on willow echo around such a huge stadium.

Having to play at football grounds brought innovation, however. With no square, Packer had to use drop-in pitches, which are, of course, prevalent today. Sometimes where the two pitches joined wasn't as seamless as it should have been and the ball could fly if it hit the line, but it was another instance of Packer using his brain to get around situations and move the game forward.

World Series Cricket consisted of Supertests – the International Cricket Conference had banned Packer from using the term Test – which would last four or five days, and one-day matches. If we played at night, we would not get back to our hotel until the small hours of the morning, completely jaded and then have to get up in a few hours to hop on a plane to fly to the next venue. This is not a complaint, I am just trying to get across that this was serious cricket and a great commitment had to be made.

Such a schedule made it tougher than an ordinary tour with West Indies. On those traditional tours we would play against state or county teams in between the international matches and we were able to take it a little easier. In World Series it was non-stop, top-class action and the will to win was huge because Packer put up prize money: in our first season we earned an extra $70,000 from prize money, which was a lot of cash in those days!

When we returned to the West Indies for a Test series against Australia, who had banned all their Packer players, we were a unit that had bonded closely during the World Series, mainly because of all the negative publicity and ire which had been directed at us. This factor, as well as the fitness work done with Dennis Waight, was crucial in making West Indies a dominant force in the years to come.

The bond was strengthened in that series against Australia. We had been aware that pressure was growing on the West Indies Cricket Board (WICB) to take action against their Packer players and they had the perfect opportunity when we went 2–0 up against a weak Australia side, which was captained by 41-year-old Bobby Simpson. Australia had refused to pick their Packer players and had lured Bobby Simpson out of retirement to take a very young and inexperienced team to the Caribbean.

I was not playing in the series because of a shoulder injury, a recurrence of the same injury that had kept me out the previous West Indies season against Pakistan in the Caribbean, but I was kept informed of the potentially combustible situation by the other players. The WICB had set a deadline for the Packer players to make themselves available for a series in India later in the year. Packer, meanwhile, was trying to negotiate with the Board to reach a compromise to allow us to play in both.

The series had moved on to Guyana at the time and a selection meeting was called that went on for hours – I think it ended at something like two in the morning. During the meeting the selectors told Clive Lloyd that they were going to drop Deryck Murray, who was secretary of the Players' Association, Desmond Haynes and Richard Austin. The latter pair were in their first series and had played well, but were also recent additions to the Packer squad. Obviously the selectors were acting on the direction of the WICB as there could have been no cricketing reason to drop the players. Cynically, the Board had picked on easy targets.

Clive demanded to know why the three were being dropped, but he was refused an explanation. Clive kept on arguing for hours without any reward and when finally he realised he was getting nowhere, he immediately resigned the captaincy. He was followed by every single Packer player in the West Indies squad, simply because we looked upon Clive as a father figure and followed him almost blindly. We just believed in him.

Not that this worried the Board. This sort of protest was exactly what they had planned for. They had back-up players, who in normal circumstances would not be considered for West Indies selection, already in Guyana for this eventuality.

None of the Packer players took part in the rest of that series, but only because of the Board and their manipulation of the selectors. Packer would have been more than happy to release us for India. In fact, during one World Series, he released Pakistani players to go to play for their country when England toured there. England refused to play against them so in turn the Pakistan Cricket Board didn't select them and I am not aware of there being a stipulation by the ICC at that time regarding official and unofficial cricket. It just showed how strongly against Packer the world's administrators were.

As it transpired, there were only two years of World Series Cricket in Australia, instead of the contracted three. Packer had finally won his television broadcast battle because they couldn't afford to be fighting against him forever. The first year of World Series Cricket had not been a success as far as spectator participation was concerned, but year two saw a dramatic improvement. Packer started to gain a stronger foothold in the Australian cricketing world and by the second year, the trust for the Sydney Cricket Ground had agreed to give him access for his games. World Series Cricket could easily be said to have been born that night at the SCG when we had a sell-out crowd for the first time. World Series Cricket and day-night cricket came alive that night. When the administrators in Australia finally decided to come to a compromise, Packer announced the cessation of World Series Cricket, paid all the players' contracts for the final year in full and walked away. Told you he was a hard-nosed businessman.

However, in the spring of 1979, there was time for a World Series season in the Caribbean. The West Indies took on Australia in front of huge crowds across the region. The series came about because of the court case that Packer had won earlier. He had won a restraint of trade against the ICC and all the cricket boards had to contribute to the costs. *All* of them, including the cash-skint West Indies who were not as uncompromising about the situation as others. Packer understood that the WICB had never really been against him and were just bowing to outside influence, so he agreed to pay their costs in exchange for him being able to stage a tour in the Caribbean. This was a tour that would be managed totally by his organisation and contracted persons in the Caribbean, and had no input from the WICB.

The series passed without incident as far as off-the-field politics were concerned. On it, however, we were less lucky. In Guyana the crowd rained bottles onto the field when play was delayed by a wet outfield. People had turned up very early in the morning, anxious to see some cricket. There was no actual rain on the day of the match itself, but the outfield was soaking wet from a previous downpour. Fans who had queued since five in the morning just couldn't understand why there was no action because the sun was shining and there was not a cloud in the sky. They got restless.

In Barbados there was a riot when Roy Fredericks was given out leg before. Back in those days, most who went to the cricket also took a radio with them to listen to the commentary. There were no television monitors to quickly look at if you missed the live action and the radio commentary enhanced the on-ground experience. When the commentator said that the ball that dismissed Fredericks had pitched outside leg, the crowd went crazy. It gave a whole new meaning to the phrase 'commentator's curse'.

The main thing I will remember about that series was the big crowds, which were in particular contrast to the small numbers in Australia that first year. The 1979 Caribbean tour was the last throw of the dice for World Series Cricket, not that we knew it at the time, but by then it was accepted fare in Australia, and the West Indian crowds wanted to see the big names and good cricket. Every Test was packed as if the traditional West Indies team were playing because all the Caribbean folk were interested in was seeing the best players play. They flocked to see the Chappells, Lillee, Marsh and the rest.

Certainly the man on the street had no qualms with the West Indian Packer players who had been previously jettisoned by the Board. Never back home did I get called a mercenary or money grabber. People understood the situation perfectly and that we had been forced out by the Board. Unfortunately though, there are a few in the Caribbean who are trying to cloud the entire Packer issue by comparing it and the players' actions to what has happened recently with today's West Indian players who have been in dispute with the Board. I can only say to them, check the facts. Some were not around then because they simply weren't born and some were too young to remember, but what took place was well chronicled; they only need to do some research.

After that Caribbean World Series leg, everything went back to 'normal'. Although it wasn't normal, of course, because Packer had changed the face of cricket forever: the coloured clothing, the floodlights, the drop-in pitches, players developing a sense of their worth. It was overwhelmingly a good thing. There are still some critics today of Packer and the players who 'did it for the money', but those people are not worth listening to because they have not done their research. If they spent a few minutes actually looking at what Packer and the game achieved, they would keep quiet. Thankfully, though, they're getting quieter as their flawed arguments fall on deaf ears.

Possibly the most important changes were players understanding their commercial value and the game itself recognising that more could be done to make it attractive to the paying supporters. And of course the administrators around the world recognising that they had a marketable product. They had to be dragged kicking and screaming out of their amateurish ways, but they eventually got there. Before, as a player, you would turn up in front of packed stands and get a pat on the back, a 'well played' and remuneration of almost inconsequence. Likewise those who were running cricket had a very amateur approach to organising tours and promoting them. Or rather not promoting them. Marketing a Test match or the game was just not done. Packer showed the entire world how to do it.

Even the unfortunate incident when the West Indians were excluded from playing was not too much of a negative. It gave the West Indies the chance to expose some new players to international cricket. One of them was a certain Malcolm Marshall, who went on that tour to India to learn how to become one of the finest bowlers of all time and help turn West Indies into an unstoppable force. Another big plus for the West Indies was the assigning to the team by the Packer organisation of a gentleman by the name of Dennis Waight, who took over the physical training and well-being of the team.

6

DENNIS

In Packer's World Series Cricket, the Australian team was assigned a physiotherapist who pretty much looked after their well-being. He seemed to know a lot more than the usual physiotherapist, dabbling a bit in amateur psychology, and was a great guy. His name was David McErlane but he was affectionately known as just 'Doc'. The West Indies then got someone assigned to their team who was in those days just referred to as a 'physio'. His job was basically to do what 'physios' did in those days, which was to run out onto the field to treat external injuries received from being hit by the ball or to try to nurse back to health internal injuries like strains and pulled muscles.

Our man was Dennis Waight, a rough and ready Aussie who hailed from Sydney. He was assigned to us thanks to Doc. Dennis and Doc were good friends so Doc recommended him to Packer. The West Indies have never had such a lucky break and the following paragraphs explain exactly why.

Dennis was to become both trainer and physio. He came from a rugby league background and I suppose because of that, cricketers could have given him a rough ride because the sports are so different. But from the first day we met him it was obvious that he was hugely enthusiastic about being with us.

Normally we would just go on tour with a captain, tour manager and assistant manager. They were at the head of affairs.

They would make the decisions. Well, now we had a trainer and it was a new experience for us. Dennis was given free reign by Clive Lloyd during World Series Cricket because Dennis had expressed surprise at our fitness levels. He told Lloyd: 'For a group of professional sportsmen, you guys are no way near fit enough.' Clive told him to do whatever he thought was necessary to get us into shape. From then on, it was a case of 'what Dennis says goes' and that wasn't just for us youngsters; skipper Lloyd was with us every step of the way. Dennis introduced a regime of running, strengthening and stretching exercises that were pretty alien to us in those days, but are the norm for the modern player. Up until then, no team involved in cricket did that kind of training. Some individuals probably took it upon themselves to do whatever training they thought necessary for their own personal fitness, but I'd never seen a whole team do it before.

Such work made us fitter and stronger than other players. There is no doubt in my mind that the work done by Dennis was the catalyst for West Indies' period of dominance that would follow World Series. Sure, we had some great talent in the team, but the level of fitness we achieved helped us to remain on the park and maintain the high level of performance over a longer period. In fact, Dennis's results with us influenced Kerry Packer to insist that the Australian team start a similar regime. Many of them were not impressed!

Of course, Dennis became a full member of the West Indies team after Packer shut down World Series Cricket. Lloyd and the players were so impressed with what he had brought to the team that he was asked to be our full-time trainer. The WICB were in full agreement. It was another salary to be paid by the not very rich board, but they saw the benefit of having Dennis around.

He went everywhere with us, whether that be island hopping

for a home series or on tours around the globe. When we were abroad he brought innovation. It was not smart to carry around dumbbells to allow players to do their strengthening work; not every airline would turn a blind eye to hugely overweight bags, and the hotels the team stayed in back then certainly did not have gymnasiums, so Dennis introduced huge elastic bands, which he referred to as 'rubbers'. They were actually the tubes you find in the inside of a bicycle wheel or in those days, inside car tyres. They would be cut into many circular bands and knotted together to a length of about four or five feet. This is what would form the source of resistance for strengthening exercises. For instance, to do bicep curls, you would place the loop at the end of the band under your foot, the loop at the other end of the band would then be held by the hand on the same side of the body. The bending and straightening of the arm against the resistance would simulate having a dumbbell instead. We could even do exercises for our legs with these bands by sitting on a chair and, depending on whether you were strengthening your thigh or hamstring muscles, have the resistance coming from in front of the chair or behind.

Otherwise, we would run. Dennis made Forrest Gumps of all of us. We just kept runnin'. The five-mile run to build strength and stamina was his trademark. It didn't matter where we were in the world, we would get on our tracksuits, or in warmer climes, our shorts, and set off. We ran through villages in Pakistan with the locals eyeing us as if we were mad, through small towns in Australia or, most ideally, a city's parkland or golf course. In Melbourne, Dennis had the quickies running up the steep steps of the stands at the MCG. My, it was punishing work, but it was brilliant training for us bowlers. Looking back now, the experts would probably say it wouldn't have been good running up and down the hard concrete steps of the MCG, but we suffered no immediate after-effects. We needed to be fitter than the batsmen because our work was more strenuous. Standing at slip and walking from end to end didn't require that extra bit of training.

Dennis didn't insist on any training that he wouldn't do himself. He was with us for every step on all our runs and he scaled those giant stands at the MCG. He was with us on our nights out, too. Dennis was one for enjoying himself and although we were able to keep up with him on the training field, he was often uncatchable at the bar.

Going out with Dennis for a late night was often a mistake because you would pay for it, not only with a sore head in the morning but with sore limbs, too. Bright and early he would expect you to be out for a run. There was no let up from the guy. He didn't feel the effects of a night out, so nor did you. 'Be up and ready to roll,' would be his words as you parted company. If he had an even bigger night than usual and looked the worse for wear on his way to bed, it wouldn't pay to believe he wouldn't be up for the run in the morning. The man had the constitution of an ox and was always, and I mean always, ready for us the next morning. In fact, sometimes Dennis would be up long before us and go for a run on his own and be back by the time we met up in the lobby to head out for our run. Then he'd run along with us again.

At times there was the odd murmur of discontent at his methods, but that's all. It is quite normal among a group for someone to get a little grumpy every now and then. Every single player could see the benefits of Dennis's regime. I remember we were in Perth once and we were all a little irritable after an overnight flight. We were on the bus to the hotel and it must have been something like five in the morning. If anyone wasn't asleep, they were certainly daydreaming about checking in and getting straight into bed. Unfortunately Dennis and Clive had other ideas. When the bus stopped in front of the Sheraton

Hotel, just up the road from a huge park that ran by the Swan River, Lloyd stood at the front and said, 'We're going to check in, then go straight to our rooms ... '. So far so good. 'And we're going to put on our tracksuits and go for a run.' Then he added with a bit of a smirk on his face, 'I know everyone is tired, but we're going to make it "one tiredness" and take the rest of the day off.' But no one complained. Okay, not everyone was happy about it, but the point is this: we all knew that it was this kind of commitment that had made us a success. Coaches often overcomplicate the game by talking until they are blue in the face about the ingredients (physical, mental and technical), but it means nothing if you do not have a group of players who are prepared to do the hard work.

Dennis and Clive chose the same lovely park by the Swan River for that run and if my memory serves me correctly, Desmond Haynes was not feeling too good. Halfway round it got too much for him and he had to stop to be sick. Clive just said: 'Keep going guys, we'll pick him up when we come round again.'

The relationship between Dennis and Clive was key, too. It was obviously based on a deep mutual respect and trust and they were very close. Clive knew that he could trust Dennis to get the best out of the guys and let him get on with it. 'It's all in your hands,' he'd say. And if Clive felt a player needed a bit of extra work, he would ask Dennis to give him some more. I mentioned how enthusiastic Dennis was when he first joined the West Indies team under Kerry Packer's World Series. Well, as time went on, that enthusiasm led Dennis to buy or acquire books on physiology and injury treatment so that he could be as knowledgeable and helpful as possible to the team. We all trusted his judgement.

Dennis therefore was considered part of the team, as important as the opening batsmen, wicketkeeper or fast bowlers. He would get a share of the prize money the team won; he enjoyed our victories and felt our failures. I suppose you could say he was an honorary West Indian. He saw it that way, too, and was keen to make sure everyone knew it.

We were in Sydney for a one-day match and Dennis had finished off some treatment with a few players in the wake of a defeat – we seemed to lose at that venue more than any other in Australia – before joining some friends at the bar. One of them said to him, 'We beat 'em good and proper tonight, eh Dennis.' Dennis replied tersely, 'Well it depends on who you're referring to as "we".'

He has been called an institution and I wouldn't disagree with that. He joined us in 1977 and was with West Indies until 2000. During these years, he missed only one tour – the one to England in 1988 because of an operation on his neck – and he calculated that one particular year, he spent 300 of the 365 nights a year in a hotel bed.

This sort of commitment showed what a professional he was. He didn't deserve to be replaced in 2000 and it all came about because the crop of players at the time weren't prepared to do the work he demanded. Dennis was a catalyst for a great period in West Indies cricket history; his departure was a catalyst for one of its darkest times. It certainly is no coincidence that since Dennis's departure, other trainers assigned to the West Indies team have complained about the lack of commitment to training and there has even been at least one resignation. He figured he was wasting his time if the players were not going to buy into the project.

After his career with West Indies, Dennis spent some time with the Pakistan team. That was a real challenge because the culture there is so different and I don't think some of the players would have been too keen on all that running. Mind you,

The bouncing baby who became known for bouncers!

I look as though I'm about to throw my toys out of the pram in this snap at Dunrobin Avenue with my sisters and brother.

Mum, who would you believe, had to drag me along to Sabina Park in my early years.

Champions. The Kingston College team in 1970–71.

A proud picture. Me with Mum and Dad in front of the Pavilion at Melbourne CC, named after my family. (Dellmar H.G. Samuels)

(*above*) Me and Dad sharing a giggle in 1995. Dad was a huge sports fan.

(*left*) Michael Manley, Prime Minister of Jamaica (Topfoto)

(*top*) Fourth Test, Australia v
West Indies at Sydney, 1975–76.
Ian Chappell is out caught by
Deryck Murray off me.
(Patrick Eagar)

(*middle*) Fifth Test, England v
West Indies at The Oval, 1976:
Viv Richards during his 291.
(Patrick Eagar)

(*bottom*) Fifth Test, England v
West Indies at The Oval, 1976.
I bowled Tony Greig in the
second innings. (Patrick Eagar)

17 August 1976: England v West Indies, Fifth Test, final day at The Oval. I take the wicket, my fourteenth of the match, of Alan Knott. (Allsport/Hulton Archive/Getty Images)

Kerry Packer and Tony Greig outside the High Court in London at the end of the first day's hearing in 1977. (Patrick Eagar)

Floodlit cricket at the Sydney Cricket Ground during the World Series Cricket Supertest Grand Final between WSC Australia and WSC World XI, 4 February 1979. (Adrian Murrell/Getty Images)

Australia v West Indies at Sydney, 1978–79. Colin Croft bowling in the first match to feature coloured clothing. A one-day night international which formed part of Kerry Packer's WSC competition. (Patrick Eagar)

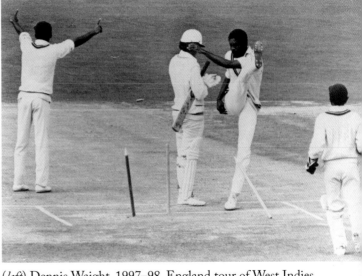

(*left*) Dennis Waight, 1997–98, England tour of West Indies.
(Graham Morris/Cricketpix Ltd)
(*above*) 9 Feb 1980: I kick over the stumps in frustration after a
decision for caught behind is turned down during the First Test
against New Zealand at Carisbrook in Dunedin, New Zealand.
(Allsport/Getty Images)

The original four-pronged pace
attack of Roberts, Holding, Croft
and Gardner which ruffled the
feathers of batsmen and pundits
alike. (Getty Images)

Malcolm Marshall, 1980
(Colorsport)

31 December 1983: Andy Roberts, the West Indian fast bowler, in action. (Allsport/Getty Images)

Ian Botham bowls during the Fifth Ashes Test at Old Trafford, 1981. England won by 103 runs. (Adrian Murrell/Allsport/Getty Images)

(*opposite page*) West Indies captain Clive Lloyd on his way to a century during the World Cup Final against Australia at Lord's in London, 1975. West Indies won by 17 runs. (Allsport/Hutton Archive/Getty Images)

(*inset*) Clive Lloyd surrounded by his players as he displays the Prudential Cup at Lord's, 1979. We had retained the Cup with a 92-run victory over England in the final. (PA Photos)

Third Test, West Indies v England in Bridgetown, Barbados, 1981. Boycott bowled by me for 0. (Patrick Eagar)

The greatest over? Not in my opinion. Sir Geoffrey will be pleased to hear I bowled quicker than when I knocked him over in Bridgetown. (Patrick Eagar)

Dennis had worked with the Somerset county side in the 1980s, so if he could get a certain Ian Botham to put his trainers on, then he was prepared for anything.

7

CONTROVERSY

They say hindsight is 20/20 vision. Looking back at unhappy experiences can bring a smile to a face that at the time held a grimace. It is always a lot easier to look back at bad experiences when you've been through them and come out the other end relatively unscathed. The 1980 tour of New Zealand was one of those instances. That's where I had my most inexcusable behaviour on a cricket field and I have to say that if that had happened today, with the ICC code of conduct now in place, I would have felt it in my pocket and missed quite a few games after the match referee had had his say.

Yes, I am referring to that stump-kicking incident in Dunedin that was so eloquently captured by a photographer who apparently didn't even know how significant a picture he had taken.

I wince a bit when I see it (really, I should have got royalties because it has been reproduced all over the world), but think it is best to try to laugh about it now. I tell people 'I lost control of my right leg' and sometimes even add the line that a football club on seeing the photo, and the height of my right foot above my head, offered me a trial. That last bit usually encouraged a laugh so that the conversation could move on to more pleasant topics.

Seriously, though, I was young and I made a mistake. I was striving to do my best for my country, but felt that the umpires in that series were not being objective. I allowed myself to think that things were stacked against me and the team, so I lashed out. Sure, it was completely the wrong thing to do but, and in no way am I trying to excuse myself here, there was so much evidence that the home umpires were making the wrong decision. Why oh why didn't the ICC think of independent umpires way back then! Mike Gatting might think the same thing when he looks back on that infamous Shakoor Rana incident in Pakistan all those years ago.

We had gone down to New Zealand after winning in Australia in 1979–80, the first West Indies side to do so. We were cockahoop and perhaps we got a bit carried away thinking that we were God's children. 'We'll walk this,' we thought. It was only New Zealand after all. If truth be known, had it not been for the umpiring we would have done. We were without Viv Richards so our batting was weaker than it could have been, but we still had a group of guys capable of beating the New Zealanders.

Dunedin was the venue for the first Test and we got the sense from ball one that the umpires were not going to be the most objective. We still thought, 'Hey, we're better than these guys, if we have to take 30 wickets to win the Test, we'll take 30.' Unfortunately we were unable to keep our cool and considering the weather conditions in Dunedin, it should not have been a problem. It was bitterly cold. As the game went on, things got worse and worse. We started to complain and of course, people started to hear that we were having a grumble. It didn't help that we were bowled out for 140 and 212 – Richard Hadlee's seven lbws were a Test record and that should be a hint as to what the umpiring was like – to leave New Zealand needing 104 to win.

I remember the radio disc jockeys talking about how they were 'gonna beat the whingeing West Indies' and that New

Zealand would get the runs with ease. That just fired us up even more and we were determined to do everything to win. We had New Zealand in trouble at 28 for two, which meant Geoff Howarth and John Parker were at the crease. This was the key partnership because after those two, the batsmen were considerably weaker. Parker was facing and I ran in, aiming just outside off stump. He moved across as if to play the ball but at the last minute decided it was best that he leave it alone. He didn't get the bat out of the way quick enough, however, and the ball took his glove, clear as day, through to Deryck Murray.

'Yes, we've broken them!' I thought as I ran through to celebrate with the team, who I'm sure were all thinking the same. I didn't bother looking back at the umpire because it was obvious that it was out and I was keen to start high-fiving everyone. By the time I got down there, Parker was still standing at the crease. He wasn't budging. I didn't know what was happening. Was the umpire waiting for Parker to walk?

I turned around in the batting crease and said, 'How is *that*?' The umpire smiled and shook his head. That was like a red rag to a bull. I just spun around and my leg kicked out at the first thing I saw and that was the stumps. Off and middle exploded out of the ground. I was livid. A close look at that same famous photo shows Parker with his bat under his arm tugging at his gloves, something batsmen tended to do in preparation for the walk back to the pavilion, only this time the umpire didn't see what we all knew. New Zealand won that Test by one wicket and the next two were drawn to send us to a series defeat.

I guess if something like that happened today, the international press might have seized on it and classed me as a bad boy or something like that. That sort of thing didn't happen back then. Not wishing to give myself a pat on the back, but I guess people didn't see me as an indisciplined character. I didn't have a reputation for unruliness and I certainly didn't gain one after the incident. It was a blip.

However, that sort of incident regarding the umpiring in New Zealand on that tour was certainly not a blip. The second Test match in Christchurch saw the same what may be termed, 'unconventional' umpiring. It got to the point where the team refused to take the field after tea on day three. Clive had reached the end of his tether and informed us all in the dressing room that he would not be taking the field with us after the interval and asked Murray to lead us out. Of course we asked him why and he told us that he was making a stand against the umpiring and would make it public afterwards, but didn't want to involve the rest of the team. This obviously occurred a long time before the Inzamam-ul-Haq action at The Oval regarding the forfeited Test against England in 2006 which, but for certain talks described in the following paragraphs, could have led to a captain taking steps outside the laws of the game, to highlight what he saw as injustices to his team.

Lloyd's reasoning was that he was close to the end of his career and was happy to sacrifice the few years left if it came to it, but didn't want us younger fellows to jeopardise our futures by following him. Now Clive was a captain and a man we all believed in and just as he stood up for us during the fracas with the board during the Packer years, we would not allow him to take the rap on his own. We all decided that no one would go out after tea.

The bell rang to signal five minutes before the resumption and as the umpires took to the field, not one of us moved a muscle. A few minutes passed, then someone pushed his head into the dressing room to tell us that the umpires were out, as he probably thought we hadn't heard the bell. He must have been the most shocked man in the world when Clive responded,

'That's fine, but we aren't joining them', with possibly a few other choice words added in.

This guy disappeared and in a flash Walter Hadlee, Richard Hadlee's father and president of the New Zealand Cricket Board at the time, appeared to ask Clive what the matter was. We and Clive simply told him that we had come to New Zealand to play cricket and what was taking place out there on the field was 'not cricket'. He and Clive left the dressing room and as far as I know, there was a meeting between Mr Hadlee, Clive and Geoff Howarth, the New Zealand captain. Apparently it was accepted that the umpiring was not up to the required standard and that as a compromise the New Zealand players would walk when they knew they were out.

When Clive returned to the dressing room and told us what had taken place, we decided to continue, but many of us had our doubts. And it didn't take long for the doubting Thomas's to be proved right. Indeed it might have been as early as the first over when another incident occurred. Colin Croft was the bowler and with the anger still boiling within, he ran in and bowled a very wayward bouncer at Richard Hadlee, which bounced well over his head. Hadlee proceeded to swat at it like an overhead smash in tennis and only succeeded in edging the ball through to Murray. We all went up with a raucous appeal, at the same time laughing at the ridiculousness of the dismissal, only to see Hadlee stand his ground and the umpire, of course, giving not out. We felt like there went that promise of fair play.

As a commentator, I know people have heard me be critical of people who have behaved badly on the field or been unsportsmanlike, and they may remember my moment of madness, but I don't think I'm being hypocritical because I would never chastise a player for his first or second indiscretion. These are inevitably commented on, but it is not the time for outright condemnation. If the player keeps on making such mistakes, only then do I really come down hard.

Thankfully, incidents like the Dunedin one never occurred again in my career and the West Indies team has never been referred to as an indisciplined team of cricketers. In fact I think it is fair to say wherever we went during that era, we were always welcomed and looked upon as a fun-loving but professional team. Another saying that emanated from my mother's lips a lot when I was growing up was, 'If you don't learn you will feel', so I tended to learn from my mistakes and indiscretions fairly quickly. Besides, I still had a mother and father who I had to face at home.

The stumps incident was one that affected me personally, but there were more controversies that we had to deal with as a team. The big one, apart from that 1979–80 New Zealand tour, which still rumbles on today, was our four-pronged pace attack. 'It isn't good for the game' was a regular cry. It makes me feel a little weary sometimes for the simple reason that I believe the criticism of our approach was based on jealousy, pure and simple. Some of the criticism that emanated from some people's lips was comical. Comments like having four fast bowlers meant the team had no balance sounded ridiculous. What is the need for this so-called 'balance' if you're winning games? This wasn't a trapeze act, it was a cricket match.

What rankles is that such views were often inconsistent. If England picked four fast bowlers against us in those days, no one would utter a word. The difference was that their four fast bowlers included men who had the long runs, but not the pace required to create the effect needed. 'Pea shooters against cannons' was how it was described by some of the press, but the principle, or idea, was the same.

It still happens. Remember the much-vaunted England side that won the Ashes in 2005? Praised to high heaven they were.

But they did it with four fast bowlers, a tactic which when employed by the West Indies was unfair or killing the game. It just proved that if a team had bowlers of the pace and quality of people like myself, Roberts, Garner, or Marshall, they would be picked to play.

Even now I get the impression people are trying to detract from what the West Indies teams of the 1970s, '80s and '90s achieved by trying to boost other teams that have done well. Of Australia they say, 'This team is better than the great West Indies side.' It started when Australia won in the Caribbean in 1995 and steadily grew. Suddenly Australia had achieved more than we did. It was nonsense. It is still nonsense.

What these people fail to realise was that between 1975 and 1995, West Indies lost only one Test series – and that was against New Zealand in dubious circumstances (I have not included the 1978 loss in India because of the ban on Packer players). This Australia team that people try to bump up lost to India in 1996, 1998 and 2001, to Sri Lanka in 1999, to India and South Africa in 2008 and England in 2005 and 2009. That's eight lost series between 1996 and 2009. Again I repeat, we lost one in 20 years and if you only take into consideration the 15 years between when we returned from New Zealand in early 1980 to when we eventually lost to Australia early 1995, the count is zero. One other thing: we didn't have the weaker Test nations like Bangladesh and we weren't even allowed to play against the then minnows, Sri Lanka.

I am not trying to disparage Australia's achievements in the last 20 years or so. They have been a great team. I am just trying to show how our achievements were decried by some because of the way we played the game. It flies in the face of the available statistics. I don't even believe in saying one team is better because I don't like comparing different eras, teams or cricketers.

To go back to our earlier theme of looking back at past problems with a smile on the face, I would concede that I am not too fond of the way West Indies played against India in 1976. It was a huge Test series for West Indies after the disappointment of the Australia tour – my first – because we were expected to win and we needed to regain confidence for the England tour. So there was a lot of pressure on us to win the last Test of the series at Sabina Park with the score tied at 1–1.

We used the drastic tactic of going round the wicket and bowling short. It was out of sheer desperation that we did it. We won, but we upset a lot of people and it was not far off from Bodyline. Many people said the pitch was to blame because there was a ridge but, in truth, we just bowled an awful lot of short balls. Sometimes the ball took off from a good length on a surface that was full of pace. Early on with the moisture still evident, it was slow. Then the sun got into it and that old Sabina gloss showed up. Man, it was quick. We went over the top and the India captain, Bishan Bedi, declared his side's first innings on 306–6 with Aunshuman Gaekwad and Brijesh Patel both retired injured and for fear of his lower order batsmen getting hurt as well. After we went past their first innings score, he again declared the second innings closed with only five wickets down. Gaekwad and Patel were still unable to bat.

Although there was a bit of a surprise when he called his guys in, Bedi was quite right. What was the point of risking injury for the sake of a few runs? Back then there were no helmets, chest guards or arm guards to help the batsmen, and himself and Bhagwath Chandrasekhar were the only ones left after Gundappa Vishwanath was also injured in India's second knock.

I wasn't comfortable with the way we were asked to bowl,

but at the same time it was country versus country and if that was what the team and captain wanted to do, then so be it. Later on, when we were a more settled unit and Clive Lloyd was a more confident captain, we didn't need to revert to such an onslaught of short balls. We were better than that and even if we came up against a tough Pakistan or Australia team, we never went back to that tactic. We wanted to win, but we wanted to do it in a gentlemanly way. We achieved that.

8

PLAYING WITH LEGENDS

Rather than dwelling on any negatives, I prefer to remember the guys I played with and the great times we had. I often get asked about some of my teammates: what they were like on the field? What they were like off it?

Most people want to know about Sir Viv Richards, or the Master Blaster, as he was known. As far as I was concerned, there has been no batsman of comparative skill, combined with mental toughness and competitiveness, that I, with my own eyes, have seen play. And I must emphasise the point about 'seeing'. I am not about to judge people I have never laid eyes on. For instance, I was not fortunate enough to see Sir Garfield Sobers and other cricketers from his era bat.

The first time I met Viv was when he was playing for the Combined Islands and I was playing for the opposition. He was a dashing and dynamic batsman who actually didn't score that many runs in that match. He just got them quickly and in superb style – 30-odd with five fours or something like that. He was a strokemaker who was yet to learn the art of shot selection.

Over time, he developed a tighter technique – both he and Andy Roberts spent some time in England, which helped them greatly – and that rare instinct of when to play a big shot or not was honed to perfection.

Viv was not one for breaking records. He played the way he

did for the team, to put us in a winning position, not for milestones. If he got a century, he was not too fussed about going on to 150 or 200 because he knew that he had done his job, which was get us to 350, and the bowlers would do the rest.

If he had wanted to, he could have gone on and got far bigger scores on a regular basis. He'd have done it easily. He would get bored, though, finding it all too easy. Just imagine if he was playing in the West Indies side today. He would have broken far more records because he would have knuckled down and got the big scores, knowing that it was what the team needed.

Often these days, batsmen are compared to Viv, which I think is unfair because he was such a unique talent. If he was in the mood, you couldn't bowl to him and it is something of a cricketing cliché but, genuinely, he had a shot for every ball. I can't really think of anyone like that around at the moment. A lot of the time on Sky Sports, the guys wax lyrical about Kevin Pietersen. I myself have mentioned him in the same breath as Viv because I think he certainly has the potential to be that good. He still has a long way to go, though, as evidenced by some of his poor shot selections that lead to what is so many times referred to as a 'soft dismissal'. If he can cure that fault and also develop some sort of a backfoot game, he has a chance. But for the time being, Viv remains streets ahead. This may seem a bit biased as he's another West Indian, but there is another batsman I would put in Viv's bracket for his technical expertise, if not his competitiveness and mental strength: Lawrence Rowe. He has been mentioned elsewhere in this book.

What few people know about Viv is that he was a dapper dresser. Still is, actually. When we were touring the world he wanted to make sure he was up with all the latest fashions. I remember he would go to a specialist shop in Sydney, down in Double Bay, to buy his shirts, which absolutely had to have double stitching on the shoulders. They say you have to look the part and Viv certainly made sure of that. He was the best and looked the best.

One of my fondest memories of the great man was when we batted together at Old Trafford against England in 1981 and he made that memorable 189 off 170 balls. The best seat in the house? I'm not too sure about that. Viv was hitting the ball so hard that day I feared for my life at the non-striker's end! The poor umpires probably felt the same. We came together at 166–9 before being bowled out for 272. My contribution? Just the 12. More significantly I only faced 27 balls.

I had come up with what I thought was a cunning plan, the bees knees, to ensure Viv would get most of the strike. The plan was that in the middle of the over, if the opportunity was only there for a single that would leave me on strike, I would only run half the way to the other end, turn around and sprint back to the non-striker's end while he ran the entire distance. The signal would, of course, come from the square leg umpire of 'one short', but that would be fine because we would still score a run and he would still be on strike. However, this plan was only feasible if the ball had been struck down to long-off or long-on where it was a long throw to get it back to the wicketkeeper. Apparently the umpires could have prevented the plan by applying an obscure law (18, note 5) which covers and prevents deliberate short runs but, of course, I wasn't aware of that at the time.

Viv didn't really look at me as I revealed my masterplan in the middle of the pitch, just nodded while he chewed ferociously on gum. I think Viv must have thought I was crazy or just thought it was too complicated to be thinking about while batting and he just kept blasting away, fours and sixes. I couldn't understand why he had taken so little notice of my brainwave. In the end I stopped thinking about it, anyway, as backing up too far wouldn't have been safe because he was hitting the ball with such force.

At the end of the innings I said to him, 'Do you remember what I said about me backing up and only running halfway to get back safely?'

'Mikey,' he said, 'I don't even remember hearing that out there. I was in the zone.'

If Viv was the best batsman I had played with or seen, then Malcolm Marshall and Andy Roberts were the best fast bowlers.

Malcolm, or Maco as he was known, made the West Indies team for the tour of India in 1978 after the Packer men were forced out. The first time I came across him was on that 1979–80 tour of Australia after the reconciliation. He was only a short guy, not even 6ft and with most of our guys well above that height, I'm sure there were a few who doubted he had pace, thinking that he would probably end up being a medium pacer like Eldine Baptiste or others of that ilk. His great friend, Desmond Haynes, told everyone: 'Don't worry, the little man has pace.' He hadn't yet made it into the final XI, but when he bowled in the nets, he was quick, quick, quick.

Much later on in his career, we were sitting down playing cards and his long pants had ridden up to his calves and I spotted he had weights strapped to his ankle. 'What are they for?' I asked him. He told me he wore them all the time when he wasn't playing, to build up the muscles in his legs. It didn't matter whether he was relaxing in the hotel or shopping, Maco would have those weights strapped to his legs. 'When you take them off for a match, Mikey,' he said, 'You feel like you can run all day.' I was astonished, but here was a young man thinking and doing that little bit extra that would enhance his career. If you watched Maco bowl, he would sprint to the crease, really pound in so his legs would get through a lot of work. But he had put in the work, his legs were so strong.

When paired with Andy, this made for a pretty intimidating fast-bowling duo and, looking back, you can't blame the batsman for quaking in their batting spikes. Andy led the attack for years and he would have gone on a lot longer if it had not been for all the county cricket he played. He and Maco both played with Hampshire, but in different eras of course.

If I was pushed to choose one over the other, maybe Maco was a slightly better bowler. Some ventured to say he was an all-rounder – he could be quite useful with the bat as England will testify when he frustrated them batting with one hand in 1984 – but I've always been of the opinion that an all-rounder is someone who could get into the side on merit for either discipline. Maco wasn't as good with the bat as that, but he was an excellent cricketer. He would swing it in both directions and he had a smart cricket brain. He is sadly missed, of course. It was very unfortunate that he died in 1999. Gone too soon.

Andy was a great friend to me and a huge influence on my career. The way he helped me with fitness issues and bowling technique made him my mentor, I guess. We met way back in the early 1970s when we were both on 12th man duty for Jamaica and Combined Islands respectively at a Shell Shield match at Sabina Park. We sat on the famous green bench in the Kingston Club pavilion and just talked non-stop about the game, probably to the detriment of our two teams, who we were supposed to be looking after.

I liked him straight away, and I got to know and appreciate Andy even more as a person when we were away with West Indies. He was a quiet, unassuming man. Some people might have found him moody and unapproachable because of that, but nothing could have been further from the truth.

Just because he was not shouting the odds or being the life

and soul did not mean he was arrogant or insular. He was a deep thinker about life and the game, and when he spoke you listened because you knew it was going to be worth hearing. That would go for criticism or advice about how to improve. If Andy suggested something you acted on it.

This 'speak softly, carry a big stick' approach benefited me time and again. In hotels and pavilions around the world, we would talk about bowling fast. On the field, too, we would have little discussions. He would come over if a batsman was proving to be particularly difficult to remove and say 'Why not try this . . .?' More often than not he was right.

Andy's class as a thinking bowler was best summed up by two instances, the first in 1983 in the home series against India. He was 32, not as quick as he used to be, and the pundits wanted him out of the team. Andy didn't listen. He took 24 wickets by outthinking the batsmen instead of blasting them away. He varied his pace, got the ball to move off the seam or flummoxed them with his slow-one-quick-one bouncer routine.

The second involved yours truly. And it was on the 1983–84 tour of India. Following a cartilage operation on my left knee in 1982, my confidence had suffered. I was tentative in putting down my left foot in delivery stride and when that happens it throws everything off kilter. Sure enough Andy spotted it. He wasn't even playing in the game concerned. He had fallen ill leading up to the first Test in Kanpur and had been left out of the final XI, but as usual he was watching keenly from the dressing rooms. His solution was to cut down my run. His theory was that, coming off the shorter run, I would have more control over my body and hence more confidence in slamming my front foot down. Well, for the first time I considered not listening to Andy. I didn't want people to think I was slacking, nor did I want batsmen to think I was beginning to lose my pace. Indeed, someone suggesting a fast bowler cut his run-up is like telling a woman she ain't as pretty as she used to be. Anyway I approached skipper Lloyd about the prospect and he just said, 'Do whatever you're comfortable with' – another instance of Lloydie being quite happy to go along with his player's wishes. Of course if he wasn't happy with the results, he would be quick to let you know!

Andy was right. I bowled off a short run for the rest of my career and after a short time I noticed I was slamming down my left foot just as much as before. It was just a mental block. Canny Andy. His help in that Test didn't end there, either. In the first innings we had India struggling on 49–6 before Kirmani and Kapil Dev started to mount a rearguard action. They had almost doubled the score when at the next water break, Andy sent out a message to me via the 12th man. He suggested that I go round the wicket to Kirmani and attack his leg stump. Lo and behold, Kirmani lost his leg stump not long after.

Of course this shortened run meant that my nickname of Whispering Death probably wasn't as relevant as before. Certainly there were a few people who were not so happy that I had abandoned my long run-up. In Barbados for the 1984 Test against Australia, the locals were most displeased. They like their fast bowlers to start their run-ups by pushing themselves off the sightscreen and when I put my marker down there was an excitable chatter.

After ball one, they wasted no time in letting me know what they thought of Holding Mark II. 'Give the ball more air, Holding!' shouted one. 'Pitch taking turn yet?' cried another. I proved my point, though. I took four wickets as Maco and I bowled out the Aussies for 97 in their second innings and we won by 10 wickets.

I only once went back to Holding Mark I. It was at The

Oval in 1984 and I did it on a nostalgic whim, which was quite out of character. Going out after tea on the fourth day I recognised a Surrey member in the crowd as I made my way down the pavilion steps. I had chatted to him following the 1976 Test when I took those 14 wickets. He said to me: 'Remember 1976.'

Now, he could well have been trying to jog my memory of our meeting back then, but I took it that he was willing me to find that same spirit. So I decided to go back to the long run for the first time in three series. Three wickets followed: Chris Broad, Allan Lamb and David Gower. Afterwards I met my friend in the crowd and we had a beer together, but I decided not to tell him that his words cost England three wickets.

9

THE GREATEST OVER

The six balls I bowled to Geoffrey Boycott on a March day in 1981 at a packed and partisan Kensington Oval in Bridgetown have gone down in folklore. They have been packaged together as 'the greatest' or 'the fastest' as it appeared I was terrorising and toying with Mr Boycott in equal measure, dismissing him for a duck by smashing his stumps with the sixth. It was pleasing to remove Boycott, not only because he was England's best and most celebrated batsman, but because we had been bowled out for 265. But the greatest over? Mercy. The fastest? No. I had bowled quicker.

I often get asked about that over. Along with those six balls – which were my first of the Test – and my 14 wickets at The Oval in 1976, they are probably the two incidents for which I am best remembered, so forgive me if I tarnish the memory slightly by suggesting that those who saw it might have got a little carried away. When people quiz me about the over it is, of course, a good feeling and I try not to tell them that those six balls were not the best of my career, or perhaps of the match.

It is difficult to categorise overs in terms of quality over such a long career, but in my mind a quicker over was one I bowled back in Australia in Perth on the 1984–85 tour. It was the first Test of the tour and I got rid of Rick Darling and Greg Chappell in the same over. I suppose it's no real surprise that in my mind my quickest over was on the then-quickest pitch in the world. My bias towards Perth could even be because that's where I got my first Test wicket, but it was generally accepted to be lightning fast.

The over to Boycott was not even my best in the match in Bridgetown. Later on in the day I dismissed Ian Botham and David Bairstow in the same over and in the second innings, I got Boycott again from my third ball. That was a special dismissal because I managed to get the ball to leap off a length and take his glove. The very next ball I bowled Mike Gatting. Two wickets in one over was better than one, surely?

I'm being a bit mischievous, though. I understand why the over to Boycott is so well remembered. It was great theatre.

The Oval was full to bursting. In fact, it had burst, with people spilling out of the stands onto the boundary edge and some were precariously perched on the roofs of the stands. There was a real sense of excitement and anticipation, heightened by our need for wickets because we had not batted as well as we should have done. There was another factor that added to the atmosphere: Boycott himself. He was always a prized wicket. A technical perfectionist, the man rarely made a mistake, so if you did get him out you always felt that you had earned your keep.

Yet that was not the whole story of what inspired me or the crowd that day. In the build-up to the Test, Boycott had made an error. He gave everyone an inkling that he was not quite in the frame of mind that had made him one of the best opening batsmen there has ever been. Ordinarily he was someone who was single-minded enough to believe that it didn't matter who was bowling or on what sort of wicket. He would always score runs. However, in conversation with groundsman Tommy Peirce it became apparent that he was not too happy. Tommy was an insurance executive with a big firm in Barbados and when he had some spare time he could be found caring for the wicket. He loved his cricket and Boycott knew him from past tours.

As usual on the days leading up to the Test match, the players would visit the ground on various days and in between practice sessions could be found milling around the pitch and on the outfield, some of them taking a deep interest in the pitch. It was not a traditional Barbados surface as there was quite a bit of grass on it.

'What's all this green then, Tommy?' Boycott asked in an irritated tone.

'That there is grass Mr Boycott,' replied Tommy. 'And in this country, it is usually green.'

Boycott went as far as to describe the wicket as a 'lottery and a farce'. The seeds of doubt had been planted in his mind. It added to the sense that something was going to happen, of that I'm sure.

As I went through my stretching and loosening exercises – I only lasted two balls with the bat so the sun didn't have too much time to warm the muscles – Clive Lloyd asked me which end I wanted. It was his way of telling me that it was time to lead the attack instead of Andy Roberts. I was taken aback because Andy was the automatic choice in my mind. He was still a fantastic bowler and had not dipped in his performances in recent series or the first Test, which we won by an innings, with Andy and I bowling nicely in tandem in the second innings.

Clive's question actually made me feel slightly uncom-fortable. Andy and I were good friends. I looked up to him and I didn't want him to think that I was trying to steal his position as the head of the attack. I told Clive 'whichever end Andy doesn't want' and he immediately understood my feelings.

Andy went with the wind and Clive said I would bowl just a

short spell of three to four overs, taking over from Andy when he had finished his spell. Knowing that, I knew I could open up the throttles and give it everything for those few overs. Andy would more than likely bowl at least seven overs, which would give me a bit of a break before having to follow him.

When a captain gives you free rein like that, it is a real boost. I came charging in and it just so happened that my first ball to Geoff Boycott was fast and on target. It pitched a couple of inches wide of the off stump – in the corridor of uncertainty, as Boycott would say. Boycott played without certainty, sort of prodding at the ball and it whacked him on the glove, falling short of second slip. It was a good start and as I walked back to my mark, I felt confident. Everything felt as though it was clicking into place: my rhythm, delivery stride, my action, my pace. It is a great feeling for a fast bowler and something that was hard to replicate regularly. Sometimes during my career I would run in with none of those factors working right.

I think the crowd could see that I was firing, so the noise started to crank up. Actually, with each ball I remember that it got louder and louder. A real din. It was rare that I noticed crowd noise because normally I would be in my own world as I walked back.

The second ball had him playing and missing and twice more before the fifth, which climbed steeply towards his Adam's apple. He fended it off with his glove again and it could easily have been the end, taken by Joel Garner in the gully, but it didn't quite carry. Incidentally, that was how I got him in the second innings.

As I was walking back to start my run in for the sixth ball with the crowd really stirred up and roaring me on, I wondered what Boycott was thinking. I decided that he would be planning for another short ball, reckoning that the crowd had got my adrenalin pumping. I had also spotted that Boycott was playing inside the line of the ball, not quite moving towards off stump as usual because it was really flying through to our wicketkeeper David Murray, who was taking the ball above his head at times. Perhaps he wouldn't move into line again. A bluff it would be then, something full and in the region of off stump.

I was right. The ball moved away a touch and Boycott was bowled playing inside the line. He hadn't shuffled right across as usual. There was almost silence as the ball moved towards its target and that satisfying crack of leather hitting the timber could be heard all around the ground just before the place erupted. Boycott's off stump cartwheeled out of the ground. It was pandemonium. Boycott looked a little confused as he walked off, looking back at his stumps as if he couldn't quite believe what had happened.

My teammates rushed to congratulate me. We were delighted to remove England's batting lynchpin and none of us really had a clue that the previous six balls would be held in such a high regard for so many years. As spectators rushed on to shake my hand, I was already thinking about the next batsman in. As I have mentioned elsewhere, you can't afford to get carried away with emotion otherwise you'd end up bowling rubbish; there was still work to be done.

Certainly down the years some of the stories about the over have not been quite right. Some people have suggested that it was a masterplan of mine to get Boycott bowled off the last ball. This is not true. You can't plan to get a guy out on a particular ball of an over. At the beginning of any over, the thought is 'good length' and 'off stump' and each delivery after that is dependent on what the batsmen did to the previous delivery. You can't think, 'I'll bowl the first three balls back of a length and then a couple slightly shorter so I can knock his stumps over off the sixth.' At least, that wasn't the case with my bowling; it was a ball by ball situation for me.

Apparently that evening Boycott, true to his studious nature, studied a replay of the over to see what he had done wrong. (I don't know where he found one because there were not television cameras at the ground like there are for Tests today and only the local network would have been covering the match.) But the story goes that Boycott pored over the footage, analysing where his feet went, whether his head was over the ball. His conclusion was that he had done nothing wrong, which was pleasing to hear. This might be a bit of folklore, but I understand that Boycott said that it was fortunate for England that he was the one on strike as if it had been anyone else, England would have lost more than the one wicket. Good old Geoffrey.

Some of his teammates and opposition members have suggested that Boycott was not a courageous player against fast bowling. I do not agree with this. He wasn't afraid that day in Bridgetown and I never detected any reluctance on his part to stand up to the pacemen in previous meetings. I remember bowling to him on a very fast and bouncy pitch at Sheffield when I was playing for Derbyshire and he played the short ball with more bravery and skill than anyone.

In 1990 I sat with Boycott in the commentary box on a Caribbean tour and during a slow period the producer decided to run replays of that over into the coverage. Boycott didn't enjoy looking back at the footage and the only time he will mention it is if someone asks him, which was a regular occurrence on those Caribbean tours. But again good old Geoffrey always had his comeback. 'I made him famous,' was his standard retort.

10

FAST BOWLER FOR HIRE

For someone who never thought he would make a living from playing cricket, I turned out to be quite the international free-lancer. A globetrotter who, West Indies and Jamaica aside, played for Rishton, Lancashire, and Derbyshire in the UK, Tasmania in Australia and Canterbury in New Zealand. As a youth I was presented a prize by George Headley at a Melbourne Cricket Club end of season presentation function. I can't remember exactly what it was for, but what I do remember is that a few weeks after that, he gave me a picture taken of me receiving the award and on the back of that photo he wrote: 'Play cricket and see the world.'

Despite George's words, I never imagined bowling fast would take me to such diverse and numerous parts of the world to play and talk the international language of cricket. Not even when I was playing World Series Cricket did I think it would be a profession. It was only an inkling. It only became a possibility thanks to Packer changing the landscape. Playing Lancashire League cricket was my first venture into professional cricket outside West Indies so let's start there.

Obviously when playing for West Indies I was getting paid, but don't forget that I still had the day job. After leaving Barclays Bank, I was dividing my time between the field of play and the Central Data Processing Unit in Jamaica (the computer department of the government) thanks to Michael Manley, the prime minister. When I got offered a job to play league cricket in 1981 I had to give up that role, as much through guilt at taking the wage when all I seemed to do was play cricket, but also because in strict terms, my job at the government computer department gave me leave with pay to represent my country. Playing league cricket for Rishton certainly didn't fall under that category. I had been in England in 1980 with the West Indies and while I was in Manchester for the Test match, which ended in a rather tame draw, Wilf Woodhouse, the chairman of Rishton, came to see me.

He wanted to find out if I was interested in playing Lancashire league cricket for the 1981 summer. Playing professionally in England had not crossed my mind since I had turned down Tony Greig's offer to join Sussex and to be honest, I thought it was something I would only do towards the end of my career, if at all. But Wilf was very enthusiastic; I liked that. He told me that the standard of cricket was good, I would not find it a chore and they only played at weekends. Wilf also reminded me of the great West Indies players who had appeared in the league down the years and the thought of following in the footsteps of the likes of Wes Hall, Charlie Griffith and George Headley certainly appealed. He said that Rishton would pay me £5,000 for the summer. In those days that was a lot of money, especially for playing at weekends only. After discussing it further I thought, 'Why not?'. In the summer of 1981 I didn't need to be anywhere with West Indies and we were not due in Australia for the 1981–82 series until December. I had all the time in the world.

I enjoyed my time with Rishton, although not the cricket. It was not as high a standard as club cricket in Jamaica and – the Lancashire Tourist Board will be gunning for me after saying this – it was forever raining. Almost everywhere I went the outfield was wet, the wickets were wet, the runs-ups were wet.

We had to put loads of sawdust down because you couldn't keep your footing when running in, so it was far from comfortable for a fast bowler like myself. I developed a niggle in my ankle as a result.

I remember turning up for an away game once and for the entire week before the weekend it had been nice and sunny. I thought, finally I'd get a dry pitch, but when I got there the square was soaking wet. Now Lancashire is not such a wet county that the rain comes from under your feet, so I think someone must have said 'Hey, that Holding's here on Saturday – get the sprinklers out.'

The only time I can remember when it wasn't soaking was a home game against Lowerhouse and I got tons of wickets, seven or eight, for very little. The pitch was dry and hard and the batsmen couldn't handle it. Lovely.

Still, the experience of the people and the whole Lancashire scene was well worth it. The first game we were supposed to play was snowed off, an incredible sight for a lad who had grown up in the heat of Jamaica. I had seen snow before, but I'd never walked through it. I'm pleased I never had to bowl through it, too.

That weekend, Andy Roberts was playing for a team at a ground close to Rishton, so Wilf Woodhouse and I jumped into the car and went over to where he was playing. It was at East Lancs, a bigger and more well-off club than Rishton. They had better facilities, pitch covers and the like. Amazingly, they were playing because they had cleared all the snow from the outfield and piled it high at the edges to form the boundary. I couldn't believe it. When I went to see Andy in the dressing room, he was huddled up by the electric heaters with what seemed like about five sweaters on and no doubt some long johns underneath.

Good old Wilf had to lend me a pair of gloves and a huge

winter coat because foolishly, coming to England in the summer, I didn't think I needed any! But then again, this was April in Lancashire. I now know a lot more about weather conditions in England. Wilf did everything to make me as comfortable as possible. So too did Eric Whalley, who was the captain at the time and he ended up as chairman of the famous soccer team, Accrington Stanley, taking them back into the football league. There was Frank the wicketkeeper, also the local butcher, who joked about playing with steaks in his gloves when standing back to me, and Betty, our most loyal supporter, whose criticism, or support, could be heard from the other side of the ground.

The people made it for me. In a small community they had folks who would turn up to cheer us at home or away. It was a nice, comfortable, warm community. Even to this day, occasionally I run across people from Rishton when I work at Old Trafford and it's always good to catch up for a chat.

With so much spare time in the week, Clive Lloyd, who was captaining Lancashire at the time, suggested I turn out for them in the odd County Championship game or Sunday League match. This was my first look at England's county circuit and it prepared me for my stint with Derbyshire later on.

Jack Simmons, who went on to become chairman of Lancashire, used to come and pick me up in his car and we formed a friendship that remains strong. He lived in Accrington, which was close to Rishton, so we would travel together when we played for Lancashire. Sometimes we had some long drives from up north to some distant southern venues, but they were never boring with Jack.

Coming back from matches, we'd stop at a pub and Jack would always have his steak and kidney pie with mushy peas or fish and chips with mushy peas. He loved his food and he was always trying to get me to eat the local fare. I would venture into the fish and chips, but I couldn't handle those mushy peas.

I understand that these days Rishton has much better pitch covers to keep the rain off. A few years after my spell with them, they signed some guy called Viv Richards and apparently crowds and bar takings went through the roof.

It was Jack who organised for me to go to play for Tasmania in the 1982–83 Australia domestic season. He had essentially become my agent, sorting out my contracts and making sure I would be looked after, although he never charged me for this help. Jack, and David Hughes, another Red Rose stalwart, would go down to Australia and play every winter in Tasmania. When Tasmania were accepted into the Sheffield Shield for the first time, they were allowed two overseas players while the rest of the states were allowed one. Jack got myself and Roland Butcher as the two to play for Tazzie in their first season. I was coming back from an operation on my knee at the time so I wasn't even sure I was going to be that fit. I needn't have worried. I performed quite well and had an absolute ball.

Early on, we went to Sydney to play the great New South Wales and won. It was a massive achievement for Tasmania, the new boys of Australia state cricket, to beat such a fearsome, well-established team. Our manager, Mr Carey, sat staring disbelieving into space after the victory. Little old Tazzie had done it. We had a few drinks in the dressing room after that victory, revelling in the fact that no one had given us a prayer. David Boon was a young man in that Tasmania team and he showed that he was just warming up in terms of run-scoring and an ability to sink quite a few tinnies.

For someone who doesn't like bad weather, I guess I picked some cold places away from home to ply my trade. But really the attraction of playing for Tasmania was purely the chance to go back to Australia, a wonderful country. Besides, it didn't hit me that I'd be away from the warm weather. I was actually based in Launceston instead of the capital, Hobart, which was something of a blessing. It wasn't as chilly as Hobart because it was sheltered from the icy breeze that rushed in from the sea. I kept on boasting that Launceston was always at least one degree warmer than Hobart. It was no Sydney or Melbourne, though.

My move to Tasmania raised a few eyebrows. Not as many as when I signed for Derbyshire though, who were not considered one of the most fashionable counties. A lot of people asked me why I went to Derby. It was simple. They asked me to. Since I turned down Sussex, no county had come in for me, and even though Lancashire were interested at about the same time, they were offering less money so I was hardly likely to be biting off their hand.

When I was down in Tazzie, Geoff 'Dusty' Miller, who played for Derbyshire and was on duty Down Under for England in the Ashes, approached me to see if I was interested in playing for them in the summer of 1983. I knew and trusted Dusty from earlier skirmishes between England and the West Indies, so I was happy to chat about it all; plus, he was at Derbyshire himself.

What I knew from seven first-class matches with Lancashire in 1981 was that county cricket was a long, hard slog. I didn't fancy playing 16 County Championship games, another 16 Sunday League games and then a handful more 50-over matches. I would not have been in the best of shape to say the least. So I suggested that I play half the county games and all the one-day matches. Derbyshire agreed. I was at the stage of my career when I was able to dictate terms, so I was happy with the way things turned out. That first season I played just the six first-class matches plus the one-day games because that was the year of the third World Cup, which consumed the early part of the summer.

This tournament may have only consumed the early part of the 1983 summer, but it consumed me and my West Indies teammates for the whole of that summer and many years after in fact. Having won the tournament in 1975 and 1979, we were hot favourites for the hat-trick. Unfortunately, we made the cardinal sin of underestimating our opponents, India, in the final at Lord's and they produced one of the great shocks of all time because they were not actually a very good one-day side.

Boy, there were recriminations in our dressing room after that loss. The bowlers blamed the batsmen and vice versa. Poor old Andy Roberts got an ear bashing from Clive Lloyd because Andy had said it was a shame we'd lost because players had given their all, even though only half fit. He was referring to me, but Clive thought Andy was criticising his decision to play when he had a muscle problem.

Things got pretty heated, so much so that in the aftermath, Clive announced his resignation before he was persuaded to think it over properly. Thankfully he carried on. Suffice to say I was glad to get up to Derby after such a crushing disappointment, one that I felt I would never get over. Time heals, though.

I made some great friends at Derbyshire and it was no coincidence that I went back in 1985 and played every season until 1989. I had a great relationship with Kim Barnett, who was the skipper. He respected fast bowlers and knew you couldn't bowl them into the ground. He kept me fresh. There was also the added joy of playing, and making friends, with fellow West Indian fast bowlers, either by birth or heritage: Alan Warner, Martin Jean-Jacques, Frankie Griffith and, of course, Devon Malcolm.

Devon, born in Jamaica, was probably the most well known

of that quartet. I would talk with Dev quite a bit about bowling fast. I've always believed in trying to get into people's heads instead of interfering with technical things. If I went into the nets with Dev, it was only ever to work on a slight technical adjustment because his action was not the sort you could mould or change for something more orthodox. He needed to be told what his strengths were and what he needed to do to be successful. Phil Russell, the coach, and Kim, believed that he could do a great deal of damage with his pace. They were proved right, with his most potent spell being when he ran through South Africa at The Oval in 1994. He had a good career, playing 40 Tests for England and, of course, the great memory of Nelson Mandela labelling him 'The Destroyer'. Not a bad story to tell.

Oh and I mustn't forget the great Dane, Ole Mortensen. Naturally we called him Stan, or Blood Axe if he was in one of his fiery moods. We opened the bowling together, although I was considerably quieter. Stan could let his frustration get the better of his emotions if things weren't going to plan and he was known to scream and shout a few things on his way back to his mark or fielding position. The important thing with Stan, however, was that he was never abusive to the opposition. Whatever ranting and raving he did was for his benefit and he controlled himself enough to do a good job for Derbyshire, where he is still loved and respected. We are still in touch and in fact he came over for a wedding in the summer of 2009. He popped into Lord's for a day at the cricket and we went out for dinner with Beefy and some other friends and had a great time.

The only disappointing aspect of playing for Derby was the fact our team wasn't all that good. Halfway through a season we'd be out of all the competitions and it became hard to motivate yourself. In the 1988 season we got to the final of the Benson & Hedges Cup to play Hampshire, but we were victims of batting first in a Lord's final when the ball would bend round corners in helpful conditions. We made only 117 and had no hope of defending it. Most seasons, though, we were out of everything by July and the last two months were a bit of a drag.

The culture off the field in county cricket in general surprised me. In 1989 I was quoted as saying that county cricketers lived off a diet of burgers and fast food. They didn't look after themselves at all. As far as fitness levels were concerned, it was like going back in time to my early days with Jamaica. There was no team warm-up. Everyone just did their own thing. I would be doing a few laps of the field and some stretches to get ready but everyone else was in the nets, reckoning a bit of a bat and a bowl would be enough. Too many players were in a comfort zone and they were more than happy to remain there. All the batsmen talked about was scoring 1,000 runs a season because that almost guaranteed a new contract from their county. That was all they aimed for, rather than getting out of that comfort zone, eating right, doing the fitness work and getting into the nets.

In my mind, a lot of players didn't even go out to try to do their best every game. Against me, Sylvester Clarke or Joel Garner, they were quite happy to get out cheaply because the next week they knew they'd be up against a less fearsome bowler and they could get the century they needed to keep the 1,000-run target on track. No problem. That would keep their numbers up. County cricket needed people to bust a gut and say, 'Hey, I'm good enough for England and I will play for them.'

John Morris was one of the county cricketers I saw who should have achieved a lot more than he did. He was at Derby so I saw a lot of him. He was a supremely talented batsman and could, no should, have scored lots of runs for England. But he didn't seem to me to have the desire to do the hard work necessary to achieve those goals and when he was picked for his country, he got in trouble with a certain Mr D Gower in a Tiger Moth plane in Australia in 1991. The good thing about John, though, was he didn't shirk his responsibilities when he came up against the 'big gun' bowlers in the opposition teams. He wanted to prove his abilities against them. I can remember one battle in particular against the great Richard Hadlee when he was at Nottinghamshire that John won and it was a pleasure to sit in the dressing room and watch him bat.

The professionalism at county level has improved to a degree through the money available to England players. Players at the highest level can make a seriously good living and the difference in salaries is a lot greater than years ago, so county players see that and aspire to it.

In the 1980s, particularly the early years, the general feeling of malaise around county cricket was blamed for England's poor performances on the international scene. I'd agree with this view. England struggled because players were satisfied with mediocrity, satisfied with their 1,000 runs or 50 wickets a season and hanging on grimly for the benefit pay day. After all, the difference in financial rewards wasn't that great and county cricket was a lot more comfortable and with less exposure to the national press. But I would also say, and this was possibly a truth that the English found hard to accept, that there just weren't very many good players around.

My one season with Canterbury in New Zealand came about through a Derbyshire connection. John Wright was a teammate of mine at Derby and also a keen adversary from clashes between West Indies and New Zealand when he was always a key wicket. As I played only half the season, Wrighty played the other half so we were job-sharing. He also loved his horses, as did Kim Barnett, so we were on common ground.

He asked me if I wanted to play for Canterbury in 1987–88,

although we would never actually play together because he was away with New Zealand in Australia for almost the entire season. It was another great experience, totally different to the one when I first toured there with West Indies when the deplorable umpiring drove me and my teammates up the wall. I got a lot more involved with the people as I was now representing the state instead of being a visiting adversary who was just there to try to beat the opposition and head home. I had a different image of New Zealand after that and I'm glad I went back. They say first impressions are long-lasting, but that second visit eased the pain of that Windies tour. The people were great and I just loved the Canterbury countryside. It was very green and I got myself a car and would drive around, taking in the scenery. The mountains, snow-capped all-year round, were a tremendous sight.

Graeme Hick was down there with Northern Districts at the time. The Great White Hope for English cricket, or so he was billed. Hick always looked good, there was no doubt about that. He was a very talented batsman. It just seemed to me that whenever the pressure was on, he didn't stand up. I remember even in that first season, he'd made a name for himself in England, gone to New Zealand and all the television cameras and press turned up for his debut. He got a duck.

Of all the domestic cricket I played in England, Australia and New Zealand, I would not hesitate to say that the Sheffield Shield was the toughest. It was so much stronger than the county game or the Kiwi scene. In England I have always maintained that the talent is spread too thinly over too many sides, in New Zealand the best players were away with the national side, but in Australia the Test players were always available.

In the Caribbean, the domestic scene was keenly fought and those wins are among my happiest memories of all the teams

I played for. We won the Red Stripe Cup in its first two years, 1988 and 1989. Jamaica had been starved of success for 21 years, so when we claimed the first of those titles, the island went crazy. It was apt that the brand new sponsors of the competition were a 'great Jamaican beer' and it certainly flowed on a lap of honour that lasted a weekend, stopped at every town and village around the island, and made the open-top bus parade that FA Cup-winning teams go on look lame by comparison.

Caribbean cricket is nothing like the other domestic competitions because it is not county v county or state v state, but nation v nation. It is fierce, often feral. Whenever on a tour with West Indies that was coming to an end, the players couldn't help but think about the battles ahead with their island teams. Jibes would start to fly and guys taunted each other, threatening total annihilation whenever one island visited the other. The Bajans would be shouting to the Jamaicans, 'You wait till you get to Barbados,' or the Guyanese telling the Trinis, 'Guyana v Trinidad is going to be spicy'. It was all in jest but when you got out onto the field for games like that, it was a serious business.

When Malcolm Marshall came with Barbados to Sabina Park one year, he got some fearful stick. He was naturally a threat to the Jamaica batting line-up and obviously pivotal in the outcome of the game. The crowd got on his case early on. They told him straight: 'When you're playing for Barbados we don't like you. When you're with West Indies we'll cheer and clap and be happy, but not this time around.' That was the feeling when it was island v island. Fierce. Very proud people.

My final first-class match in the Caribbean was against Barbados at Kensington Oval. We needed a draw to win the 1989 championship and we duly got it, not that I helped a great deal with the bat. I was out off the bowling of Desmond Haynes would you believe, who couldn't stop laughing as I made my way back to the pavilion for the last time. As you may have guessed since Dessie was bowling, fortunately by this time the draw had already been guaranteed and the job done.

11

TIME TO GO

By the time of the 1986–87 tour to Australia and New Zealand, my career had come full circle. I had, of course, made my first international appearance for West Indies Down Under in 1975 and had such a miserable time with players forming cliques and backbiting that I considered quitting for good.

Well, when it all happened again more than ten years later, with me being a wise old sage at the age of 33, not to mention not quite the tearaway fast bowler that I used to be. I was sure this time that I had had enough. I wanted out of international cricket.

We were to play two one-day tournaments in Australia before heading off to New Zealand for three Test matches and another series of ODIs. The tour started badly and got worse. Firstly we flew into Australia on Christmas Eve night so we arrived in Perth on Christmas morning. Can you imagine players agreeing to that these days? The mood was not enhanced when we discovered that Viv Richards, the new captain after replacing the retired Clive Lloyd, had been allowed by the Board to spend Christmas at home before flying out later, hardly a boost for team morale.

Already you can see the similarities between this tour and my first: a new captain learning on the job, just as Clive had been, about how to deal with individuals and the discipline of the group as a whole. Clive didn't get the balance right on his first tour so it was not a surprise that Viv didn't quite manage it, either.

At the time I believed much of the difficulty surrounded one of our senior players, Gordon Greenidge. Gordon was struggling with a knee injury and he wanted a rest, saying he was stale from so much cricket. He was essentially refusing to play on fitness grounds, but we were desperate for his experience (Desmond Haynes was out with a broken finger) for a World Series Cup game against England in Devonport, Tasmania, a game we had to win to qualify for the finals.

We had grown accustomed to Gordon and his injuries, but it was unusual for him to not play at all. He was famous for limping and hobbling around at the crease. So much so that it had become a joke. I remember once in Sydney that Gordon was limping so much, it looked as though one leg had fallen off. Andy Roberts, whose cousin was married to Gordon, said: 'I'd love to see him if this building ever caught fire.' And by the way, they used to say that when Gordon Greenidge started limping, bowlers should watch out. That was no myth. He truly was at his most dangerous whenever he appeared to be struggling. Under normal circumstances, team members would have just ignored him and got on with playing, but this time around there was some mutual animosity between him and the rest of the team. It was simply because we were losing and needed his skill and experience.

We were beaten seven times in 11 one-day matches in Australia. It was hardly the ratio we were used to and our problems were a big story in Australia, with the locals baffled by our change in fortunes. When the newspapers start to revel in your demise, players have injuries and there is lots of squabbling in the camp, it is hard to break the cycle. As a result, players lose focus on their cricket and turn their attention to some of the other activities that a country like Australia can offer. That is the challenge of touring.

I found it all immensely frustrating because I was vice-captain but powerless. For example, Viv, Steve Camacho, the manager and myself were the tour selectors and we had to make the decision as to whether Gordon was fit enough to go to New Zealand at the end of the Australia leg. We agreed he was not, and although he was a very fine player, that he should go home. He hadn't been fit to play in Australia and there was no point in him limping around New Zealand as well.

So I was surprised that Gordon did come to New Zealand, having left the meeting under the impression that a replacement would be called for. I was pretty fed up. There was no cama-raderie among the guys to lift me, or anyone else, out of the gloom and that was not how cricket tours should be. I even seem to remember a couple of guys coming close to fighting each other over some trifling matter.

Discipline had broken down. I called the chairman of selec-tors Jackie Hendricks back in Jamaica and told him that I wasn't comfortable with what was happening; certain cliques were being formed within the team, which wasn't healthy, and that I wanted him to take the vice-captaincy away from me. I argued that vice-captaincy on tour was a very responsible position and that with what was happening around me, I didn't feel motiv-ated enough to put in the effort required for the job. In other words, I just wanted to complete the tour as an ordinary player without any extra responsibilities and call it a day at the end. By this stage I knew this would be my last tour and I just wanted to go out there and try to take wickets without the responsibility of making sure so-and-so were getting along okay or this guy wasn't sulking or what have you. It was probably not the ideal way to go about it. I don't want to say it was the cowardly thing to do but probably selfish was the right word.

I just felt that I was powerless to do anything about our problems. However, Hendricks didn't let me give up the role. He thought the team needed my support. Since it was my last tour he thought I may as well keep it.

My exit from the international stage came quicker than I expected though. We had muddled through the one-day action in Australia and had headed out to New Zealand with many of the issues still unresolved. During the first Test I developed a back strain. It was nothing too serious, just a twinge, and I spoke to Dennis Waight about the injury. 'Not a problem,' he told me. 'You'll be back in time for the one-day series at the end of the tour.'

Well, I didn't get into cricket to play one-day matches. I enjoyed them and I played in them because they were there, but Test cricket was what it was all about. So if I was not going to be fit I thought it best that I go home and let someone else have a go.

It was not a serious injury at all. It was just a little strain from perhaps landing badly on delivery and could easily have happened in my first Test as much as my last. I suppose what I'm trying to say is that the injury played no part in my decision to retire; it just brought it forward by a couple of Tests. I didn't think, 'I just can't go through another rehabilitation period' because it would not have been a long, painstaking process, a train of thought which many players have cited down the years for their decision to call it a day.

I had become used to these sorts of niggling injuries because I was not a big, strong powerful guy, and trying to bowl fast with a reasonably light frame would always involve a few injuries along the way. I lasted as long as I did because of my nice, smooth action, which didn't take a lot out of me. I got a knee injury, lateral cartilage removal, back in 1981–82 right after a series against Australia and had it operated on in February

1982; also I had shoulder problems through a torn rotary cup in 1976, but otherwise most of my knocks were pretty minor. The niggle I got in that first Test in New Zealand, which happened to have started four days after my birthday, was just another small one. It just made me think that I may as well go straight away as opposed to waiting until the end of the series.

I went to Steve Camacho in the dressing room after I'd come off the field and told him, 'Dennis says the injury's not going to heal to play the rest of the Tests and I think it's better for me to retire, go home and you can find a replacement.' Steve was shocked at how blunt I was being over such a big decision. 'Mikey, are you sure about this ... think about it for a while.' I told him I'd been thinking about it for a couple of years.

In fact, I had wanted to retire back in 1985. Jackie Hendricks had convinced me not to. West Indies were going to Pakistan and he told me to miss that tour to think about things and then only pack up if I still felt the same. I carried on because that time off refreshed me. So it was no spur of the moment thing.

'I think I need to go home,' I repeated to Steve. He knew I was serious then. We were not tucked away in the corner of the dressing room whispering to each other, but talking about it openly. Some players could hear what we were saying and the rest heard about my decision later. I was never one for big announcements so I certainly didn't stand up in front of the guys and make a speech. 'Excuse me gentlemen, I've got something to say' – no, not me at all. The news just filtered out.

Steve made the arrangements for me to go home. I was happy about the circumstances, if you can be happy about something like that. I went to New Zealand with 249 wickets and I walked out of Test cricket with 249 wickets. I didn't bowl well enough in my last Test to take a wicket, although that had a bit to do with the injury, just like I didn't bowl well enough in my first to get one in Brisbane in 1975. Full circle.

After it was finally confirmed and made public that I had retired and was heading home from New Zealand, I was extremely thankful that I did not take that wicket to get me to 250. That may sound strange, but I am happy that I did not get a wicket because in the end people would have said that I only went on that tour to get to or pass the landmark. I didn't want that thrown in my face.

When I jumped on that plane, the overriding emotion I felt was not one of sadness or despair, it was pure relief. It was all over. No more training runs, which initially were enjoyable, but had become a bind and only done because it was necessary; no more pounding in for over after over and certainly no more having to listen to pathetic squabbling from teammates. Never did I worry that I would miss the game. I wasn't enjoying it any more. That was the bottom line.

It was a similar situation when I retired from first-class cricket. I played two more years with Derbyshire and Jamaica after retiring from internationals. I knew it was the end when, one morning in Derby I got out of bed at home and went to the curtains. Pulling them back, I felt deep down inside that I was hoping that it would be dark, raining, with little chance of play. When I caught myself doing that I said to myself, 'If this is how you feel about the job you're doing, then don't do it.' I don't believe in doing something that you're dreading doing. You've got to look forward to a job when getting out of bed in the morning. I think this feeling comes to fast bowlers much quicker than it does batsmen. Bowling quick is hard work physically and mentally and we bowlers were always clambering out of bed feeling an ache or pain somewhere. I often found that I was going into a game nowhere near as fit as I'd have liked – that took its toll mentally and physically. So I was ready for both retirements, international and first-class.

Not that most of the people on the street agreed, but then

they rarely do. In the ten years after I packed up, people kept telling me I retired too quickly. My answer was: better to leave early and to be told so by the fans than to hang around too long for those same people to say, 'What you still doing here?' Never overstay your welcome.

The timing was fine. West Indies still had a lot of fast bowlers to choose from: Malcolm Marshall was at the top of his game, Joel Garner was on that tour, there was Tony Gray, who replaced me in New Zealand, plus Patrick Patterson, Courtney Walsh and Winston Davis. So there were quite a few guys who could carry the mantle. I was not leaving a team whose cupboard would have been bare without me.

Of course, Courtney would go on to play 132 Tests for West Indies, taking a fantastic 519 wickets in a career spanning an incredible 17 years. He is probably the most durable fast bowler there has ever been. Not bad for a guy who I remember as a kid in Jamaica (we came from the same club and are both still members) who started off bowling leg breaks.

I first thought of retiring when Clive Lloyd retired and I suppose I felt that I should go at the same time. He was such a huge influence on me and when he was no longer around, something wasn't quite right. We had been through a lot together and I owed him my career. He was the guy who believed in me enough to pick me as a bowler who had only shown promise, he thought of me in 1977 when I hadn't been actually playing, got me into World Series Cricket and he was the man, of course, who led us to such great success on the field.

I've already said this, but Clive was a father figure. When I carried on playing for a couple more years without him, it simply wasn't the same. I was enjoying it to a degree, yes, but it wasn't the same feeling. Although Clive had been incredibly inspirational, it wasn't a case of not being able to raise my game or go at full tilt anymore – my motivation was the West Indian people, who relied on you lifting their lives, and this was always stronger than anything an individual could say or do. It is hard to explain what it was like with Clive no longer in charge. This comparison shouldn't be taken too literally, but it sort of illustrates what I'm trying to say. In life, your parents die and life goes on, but it has a different feel. You still have to go out and do whatever you did before, BUT IT'S DIFFERENT.

It was also important that West Indies moved on from Clive and for Viv Richards to move on with his own team. Viv said that in his first team meeting. 'Clive is gone, I'm the captain, I'll do it my way.' It wasn't said to mean that any policies in place would drastically change, just that he was a different personality and things would be different. Viv became a very successful captain, but he was a completely different type of captain and it was something of a culture shock.

Viv was very competitive, just as Clive was, but it manifested itself in his reactions to anything below the standards he expected. He wasn't as understanding as Clive. Viv wouldn't accept some of the frailties that Clive put up with as far as performance was concerned. Viv was such a good player and so fiercely competitive that he initially found it difficult to contain his emotions when mistakes were made. Of course Clive was also very talented, but he knew players would make mistakes, it was part of the game and he controlled his emotions accordingly, at least the vast majority of the time. But despite their differences, both were great captains.

Indeed, Viv has a brilliant record as captain, but sometimes Viv's temper could get the better of him. I would see him come down so hard on some youngsters, especially those from Antigua, his homeland, that they would struggle. It was almost as if they were disappointing him and he had to let them know. When you're a young impressionable guy and someone like Viv is telling you off it is natural to think that he doesn't like you or is picking on you. It was not the case. In fact, the opposite. He wanted them to do well really badly.

It was a bit like when I'm commentating and am very hard on West Indies. It's not because I don't like them, but I still feel a part of West Indies and when they don't do well, you can be too harsh. Their success still means a lot, you're upset and you're not taking a totally neutral view. That was happening with Viv. His emotions were getting involved with the players not living up to expectations. I'm not talking over a whole career; it was in an instance: a dropped catch, bad over, misfield, a poor shot. Little things like that. It was hard having been used to Clive, but I told myself, 'As he grows in the job it will change.'

Viv's emotions didn't affect me too much because I was a senior man. I saw how the youngsters reacted to the pressure they were under and that sort of thing. However, one instance of this did involve me, in Gujranwala in 1985, when we were playing a one-day international against Pakistan. Imran Khan was batting and he was taking the game away from us, whacking the ball to all corners. Joel Garner was bowling and he was going for a few boundaries, so Viv game me a nod to replace him.

We had a packed leg-side field, maybe a 5–4 split with Viv at short-midwicket. My first ball was on the legs and Imran just whipped it away, going over Viv's head and bisecting the fielders on the boundary for four. Well, Viv had a look on his face that sort of said, 'Oh, so you're going to bowl rubbish too, then?' I didn't want to bowl to a heavy legside field. I wanted it changed and I motioned to Viv to switch it. But he still had this look on his face and was completely ignoring me. So I just stood there, with hands on hips at the end of my mark, not budging. Effectively I was refusing to bowl until he took notice of me. It was a bit of a stand-off, but in the end he relented and came over to discuss the change. This time we went for an offside bias. Next ball Imran sliced one straight to Roger Harper at backward point and he took the catch.

Clive and the cliques in the team were not the sole reasons for my retirement. Thanks to my age, the niggles I'd suffered and my reduced run-up, I was down to 75–80 per cent from my peak in terms of effectiveness. That was hard to reconcile. I was not the bowler who destroyed England at The Oval any more. Geoffrey Boycott called me the Rolls Royce of fast bowlers, but I was by now a considerably less grand machine. At this stage, I wasn't going into a Test thinking, 'I'll take five or six in this Test.' I was no longer a lead bowler. Indeed, I was second change in that first Test against New Zealand. This was not something I wanted to be and I didn't look forward to doing it.

How do I look back on the career I had? I have never really thought about it very much. I'm not one who sits at home and pours over the old scorecards, reminiscing how I got so-and-so out, I haven't even got a cricket picture on any wall at home and I don't look up old footage on YouTube. I was even reluctant to write about the 'Greatest Over'. I was never even someone who thought about 'my career' when I was playing, apart from taking 'my wickets' to make sure I was selected. I was only around to help the team and to help West Indies do as best they could. I wasn't focused on me. That was why I was so glad I didn't get the 250th wicket. I didn't want people to think I thought it was about me. Actually, that's the only time I do hark back at my career, to remember how fortunate I was that I didn't achieve that figure!

It was all about the team, and there were many memorable team results. The World Cup win in 1979 was great – it was the first time I was involved in a world tournament – but Test cricket was the ultimate and I cherish memories of being part of a team that was the best in the world. The highlight was probably winning in Australia, 2–0 in a three-Test series, in 1979–80. It was all the more special as it took place on our first tour back in traditional cricket after Packer. It was also the first time West Indies had ever won a Test series in Australia, or even won more than a single Test. We played such good cricket, too. In Melbourne we were dominant, winning by 10 wickets and in Adelaide we were more so. The 408-run margin victory was at the time the sixth-biggest win in terms of runs. It is still number eight today.

I do recognise that I was a lucky sort to have lived the life of a cricketer. Being part of a great team made a big difference; we earned a lot of respect all over the world. We'd go to Australia and have Australians wanting West Indies to beat their team because they loved the way we played. When that happens, you think hell, that's great when you get to turn home supporters. That's some power. And I'm not talking about the odd few, I'm talking about thousands.

The guys would joke about our charmed existence, this spoilt life . . . how we'd wake up in the morning in a fine hotel, shower, disappear out of the room to play cricket or go shopping, and when we got back everything was spic and span, the bathroom cleaned, beds made. (As kids in the Caribbean when we got up in the morning, we couldn't go out to play until the bed was made and other household chores were completed, parents watching over us!) We knew it wouldn't last forever but we made hay while the sun shined.

12

ON THE GAS

I want to use this chapter to say a big 'thanks' to the Jamaican people who supported me when they didn't need to, who gave me help when they had nothing to gain from it and, believe it or not, those who put their lives on the line with no reward coming their way. They did it for me, and when I sit here writing these words, it makes me feel very humble indeed as to the lengths folks went to.

Having retired from first-class cricket in 1989, I went back to Jamaica needing to make a living. Many options were considered, but it transpired that I would end up running a petrol station, 'Michael Holding's Service Centre', and it was in this venture that so many people bent over backwards for me.

I can't quite recall how I eventually settled on this course of action, but Howard Hamilton, who used to be head of Shell in the Caribbean, and a friend of the family since he went to school with my sisters, was the catalyst. Howard and I had become pretty close. He took an active part in cricketing matters in the Caribbean because Shell sponsored the regional Shell Shield tournament in which the islands and regions competed for first-class honours and so formed friendships with many Caribbean cricketers. As time went on over my playing career, we became very good friends and even part-owned horses together.

I either went to him with the idea or he suggested it to me.

Either way, the timing was perfect because there was this Shell station in New Kingston that the gentleman running it was looking to sell. There were a lot of positive vibes in the move. The gentleman was Alwyn Miller, an ex-Kingston College student like myself, and Howard helped me to negotiate with him to buy the station. I took over the accounts a few months before the first Gulf War and immediately the price of petrol went sky high. The windfall was instantaneous because although the purchase price went up, the actual mark-up to arrive at the selling price was a percentage of the purchase price, not a flat amount. It wasn't a bad time to take over the business. 'What an easy lark this is,' I reckoned naively.

At the time there was another gentleman, Guy Morris, who also had a Shell petrol station, and was also a big cricket fan. He offered to help me set up the business. I sat down with him at his station with our respective managers to go through the business before the formalities were completed. Step by step he taught me how to run the show, the systems, how everything should tally up and what I had to do with the books. When I started he even went on to lend me a couple of his staff to train mine because they were brand new to the business. Guy did not have to do that for me. After all, it could be argued that we were rival stations, as we were not separated by more than a handful of miles.

By the time we were into full swing at Michael Holding's Service Centre, my full complement of staff numbered twelve. It was at the time when each pump needed an attendant. Most of them came from Melbourne Cricket Club, where I played my formative cricket and remain a member for life. We had a lot of youngsters from the area who didn't have jobs and so I brought them on board because I knew they were reputable people. I had two girls there, as well, who were the children of the first helper that I had to look after my youngest daughter,

Tiana. Pearl, as she was known, loved Tiana, Tiana loved her, and she was someone we could trust implicitly. I took them on because I knew Pearl and her family had to be good people. They all worked hard for me and we had a great relationship. Of course over the years I employed some people who I did not know and inevitably some of them didn't last in the job. Suffice to say, when there is cash around, the temptation can be too great for some to endure.

It was hard, rewarding work. Often non-stop, too. For the first eight or nine months at that station, I spent 18 hours a day there. I was there morning, noon and night. The only day I wasn't there the entire time was a Sunday. On weekdays, Monday through Saturday, we would have two eight-hour shifts, and they would overlap, starting at 7 am. I had to get there before the first shift and I was there when the second ended at 10 pm. On a Sunday we just had one eight-hour shift starting at 8 am. Before the day's sales started, the level of petrol in the underground tanks had to be measured, correlated to what had been measured the night before when locking up and at the end of the day, measured again. The difference then had to correlate to the volume of petrol sold according to the records of the attendants. Not all reconciliation was done that night, but my office work didn't end for me the moment the pumps outside were shut off.

I remember one New Year's Eve, with the same supposed 10 pm lock-off time, I was trying to close the station to get back home to be with friends and family, but I couldn't. Cars just kept pulling in. We closed the majority of the pumps, but each time I even attempted to close down the final pump, in would come another car because they knew it would be their last chance for petrol for a couple of days. I got frustrated that night, but that was the nature of the business, and the staff who were there just rolled along with what was happening.

Eventually we got a break and closed the remaining pump, rushed inside and turned off the outside lights and got down to the bit of paperwork necessary before we could all head home. I would usually drop home as many of the staff as I could each night as getting public transport that late wasn't easy. That night none of us got home before midnight so I wasn't able to say cheers and happy new year, but those were the sacrifices I had to make. It was nothing in comparison to the ones the Jamaican people made for me ...

Michael Holding's Service Centre was at a very awkward spot on the corner of Trafalgar Road and Knutsford Boulevard, which formed a T-junction with Trafalgar Road forming the cross of the T, making it difficult to get into the station. Drivers heading east on Trafalgar would have to cross two lanes of traffic heading west, to fill up. Those heading north on Knutsford Boulevard, had to turn right, heading east, onto Trafalgar, then cross the two lanes heading west to get into the station. There were a lot of accidents, the sound of the crunch of metal being such a regular occurrence that after a while it stopped making me jump out of my chair. Sometimes the car turning into the station would start to make its way across because the car on the outside lane heading west would stop. But the person on the inside wouldn't and not being able to see in front of the stopped car, they would collide. Believe me, I can't say that I would be risking going into a station three or four times a month if that was the problem. The only completely safe direction to be coming from was going west on Trafalgar Road.

But the people of Jamaica supported me and although there were prangs, people still kept those cars rolling in. A lot of businesses in the New Kingston area came and opened accounts. Some of them closed accounts at the two other stations within New Kingston to open with me. Others not even in the immediate area moved their accounts over.

It was not only the bodywork of their cars that Jamaicans risked. Some put their lives on the line. With all the cash involved I would have to go to the bank every night to deposit the takings. A risky operation, no matter where in the world you worked. But again, people came good. I had a friend in the police force who used to visit me before I could afford to hire a security company to deal with the money. This guy would wait for me every night and make sure I got to the bank safe and sound. Eventually he was transferred from Kingston to St Thomas and was no longer able to be my personal security guard. But do you know what he did? He called a colleague of his and told him, 'You've got to help Mikey.' I had never met this guy, but every night he was there without fail. We formed a great friendship. He would come before the station closed, have a chat and then escort me to the bank. And if I wanted him to follow me home he would do that, too.

Above and beyond the call of duty, that's what you could call it. There was no need for those guys to do that and they never asked for a dime. We never knew if there was a man with a gun waiting for us to lock up and then strike, making off with the takings or worse. I won't mention the names of these two policemen because I am not too sure they would want me to, but gents, you know who you are and THANKS again.

It was amazing. I knew that I had done reasonably well at cricket and had grown accustomed to people calling out to me in the street, either those that I knew personally or those who just recognised me passing by, but that's about as far as I expected the relationship to go. With some it went a lot further. Possibly their help was because I'd given them pleasure through my cricket and maybe they were repaying me, not that I needed it for I certainly enjoyed it myself. I played for successful teams and I guess people get attached to you because you've given them joy. But that doesn't mean they're going to take risks for you like those policemen did.

Overall, I would say that I had no regrets about running the gas station. It was a great learning experience. You can become a little insular or cosseted as a cricketer, so the benefit of getting back into the real world was huge. Most of all, I learnt about people, how best to manage my staff and how to treat both staff and customers. They were always right, of course, but sometimes even dealing with some of them was a little trying. For example, the odd person would come into the station and try to do something that would make you think 'Why?' Somebody with a business account approached me once to do what is called double invoicing. I was supposed to supply two invoices for petrol and services rendered. One was the correct invoice that would be paid and the other would be much higher for them to use to claim back on income tax. There was no way I was going to get involved with such a scheme because I didn't want people knocking on my door. I advised the account holder as such and to be honest, there was no argument from the person, no hard feelings held; the situation was accepted and never mentioned again. I guess it was just someone trying to see how far I was willing to go to help them with their endeavours. Episodes like that certainly opened my eyes to the business world and taught me a few things about human nature.

I also learnt what real strenuous hard work was. I thought fast bowling was tough on the body, but this was real stress, physically and mentally. As I mentioned earlier, I spent a lot of time on site in the formative years and the hours were draining. It wasn't always as rosy as it first seemed when I first started either. Running a petrol station has its trials and tribulations, for example, finding that you're selling less petrol than you supposedly bought! Once when things were not going that well, I can remember going to see one of the supervisors at

Shell who would be responsible for my station and almost breaking down in front of him because I was finding it so stressful. I then started to do radio and television commentary work away from Jamaica and that didn't help either.

There is an age-old Jamaican saying that goes something like this: 'The eyes of the farmer fatten the cow.' Which simply means, the business flourishes the more the owner is around.

However, the point came when I could no longer cope. With my commentary career taking off, I was spending less and less time at the station. When I was in England in 1995 working for Sky Sports, I was away for four months and that just wouldn't do for a manager. At least not me. I wanted to be involved in the station, not just own it and employ people to do the work.

To make everything run smoothly, there was a multitude of things that needed to be done and without me there, it was a bumpy ride. I had a wonderful lady called Mrs Wint who worked for me in the office and in my absence she was in charge. She was honest and hard-working, but unfortunately she was too nice. The staff recognised that she could be a soft touch so those who wanted to, took advantage, slacking off from their work. Mrs Wint couldn't quite demand the respect she deserved.

On that trip with Sky, I called home one day and asked to speak with my mother, just to catch up with the family news and tell them what I was up to. But she wasn't there and I was told she had gone down to the gas station. Now my mother didn't drive and had never held a driver's licence in her life, so she hadn't gone to fill up her car.

'Why has she done that?' I asked.

I was told that she was down there helping out because of the problems, trying to organise people, checking the books and what have you. This was 1995, so Mum would have been

81. I felt embarrassed and angry that she was having to help me out with my responsibilities at such an age. It just wouldn't do and I made the decision immediately to sell the station.

So by June 1996, Michael Holding's Service Centre was no more. Today there isn't even a gas station on that precarious corner of Trafalgar Road and Knutsford Boulevard. The gentleman I sold it to kept it as a station for a while, but didn't do too well and it was later sold to a bank who turned it into a parking lot. The bank that bought it has played a large part in my life. It's the same bank where I got my first proper job in the computer centre after leaving school. I then had my personal and business accounts there as it was in such close proximity to the station. The name had changed over the years from Barclays Bank to the nationalised National Commercial Bank, but it was the same physical structure.

13

BEHIND THE MIC

Grumpiness can often be mistaken for concentration. That was my excuse anyway. On the field of play, my occasional fondness for a furrowed brow and a scowl must have led many watching at home to reckon that I was a miserable so and so. I came to that conclusion because the cameramen who were filming those shots told me exactly that. A lot of those same cameramen are still around today and, unfortunately for them, my face is still filling their lens, although in a different guise as commentator.

'We used to zoom in on you when you were playing, Mikey, and you never looked the happiest,' one told me when we were working together for Sky Sports. 'It really surprised me that off the field you couldn't have been more different.'

I was glad for such a compliment because the last thing on my mind when playing was how I was being perceived by viewers, but the first thing on your mind as a commentator is, obviously, how you come across. Richie Benaud famously said, 'Remember you're in people's living rooms, let them feel happy to have you there,' or words to that effect anyway, and I've always respected his opinion on things like that.

It would be my hope that in my 21st year as a broadcaster, people no longer think of me as grumpy (although I have been known to get a little cross in the comm box every now and again), and instead that I help them to enjoy the action. It is a cliché but truly, all broadcasters, whether on radio or television, are guests in people's homes. I am incredibly grateful for their invitation and acceptance. A career in broadcasting came along at just the right time. It allowed me to extricate myself from my gas station business and has given me the financial security that I had hoped for.

This may not come as a surprise to you given the earlier passages about my burgeoning career as a cricketer, but just as I never had an ambition to bowl fast for West Indies, nor did I have a passion to forge a living from broadcasting. My timing was perfect as a cricketer in terms of being around at the right time for the Packer revolution – the same was true as a broadcaster. I was respected enough to be in demand from the likes of Channel 4 and Sky Sports just when a bidding war was underway for the broadcast rights to English cricket.

It could all have been so different. After hanging up the bowling boots, I tried my hand at running the gas station and I dabbled with umpiring. Dabbled is the right word because I did not want to do it professionally. My interest was sparked by my experience as a bowler. I wanted to know what it was like to be the man standing at the wicket with the bowler behind, motionless, focused and poised to make all the decisions. Or in other words, if you'll excuse me a moment for slipping into fast-bowler mode with a furrowed brow and scowl, I wanted to know whether it was as hard as some umpires made out. Did it get tiring? Was it boring? Why were so many mistakes made? Throughout my career I struggled to accept poor decisions and there was a part of me that was still struggling to comprehend why I didn't get some of those decisions that were so blatantly wrong, for example, in the Sydney Test in 1976 or the infamous one against New Zealand in Dunedin in 1980.

The aim was to umpire a few domestic games in Jamaica to find out for myself how difficult a job it was. To that end I spoke with Johnny Gayle, who was head of the Jamaica Umpires Association, about taking the necessary qualifications. Alas, with the gas station taking up much of my time and a broadcasting career beginning within fourteen months of my retirement, I never found the time to excuse all the umpires who had denied my appeals when I was so convinced that I had claimed a wicket. I guess those questions will remain unanswered in my mind.

The umpires were let off the hook thanks to a man called Ed Barnes, who worked as a producer for Radio Jamaica (or RJR as it was known). My memory fails me when I try to remember when Ed and I first met, but we got along famously because of a shared love of sports and horseracing in particular. He followed in the footsteps of his older brother Winston, who was among the best broadcasters and radio personalities Jamaica has known, and commentated on all the sports, including races at Caymanas Park, a real skill, and we would spend much of our time discussing the sport.

During our chats Ed realised that I was not quite as stern-faced as I was on the field. I suppose he must also have spotted something that he thought would make me a reasonable radio broadcaster. Never have I tried to guess what that was, however. Anyway, Ed asked me whether I fancied having a go at some cricket commentary for RJR. I told him I didn't. I had never thought about doing it and, honestly, I wasn't sure whether I had the ability.

'I don't want you to describe the action ball-by-ball,' he told me. 'I just want you to speak every now and again, giving your analysis of what is happening.' In other words just adding colour with my comments in between overs. This argument did not convince me, either.

'Look, I've never done public speaking,' I told him, insisting it wasn't for me.

Of course, I had public speaking experience of a sort. As a player I was always happy to do interviews. I often spoke freely, too freely for some as it happens. After the Test match against India in Trinidad in 1976, I caused a bit of a stir. India had chased down what was then a world-record fourth innings target of 406 and they were cheered on by Indians who had been born and bred in Trinidad. I couldn't understand that and didn't think it was right. Surely they should have been supporting us? I was approached by someone from the press who didn't identify himself and asked for my thoughts. I told him that I felt it was like being in Bombay and my comment made headlines. Fancy that, me saying exactly what I thought as way back as 1976.

Ed would not take no for an answer. Over the next few days he kept calling me, pestering me to do it. Eventually I relented and my first spell behind the mic was for the first ODI between West Indies and Pakistan in Jamaica on 12 March 1988. What had changed my mind? Well, I knew that Ed would be there, as well as my friends Tony Cozier and Reds Perreira, who would be doing the ball-by-ball stuff. With familiar faces around, and people who were very good at their jobs, I thought it wouldn't be too intimidating.

I remember being anxious on that first morning, although thinking back to when my debut for Jamaica was spoilt by nerves, it wasn't nearly as bad. Playing sport at a high level helps you deal with pressure and in relation to performing in front of a large crowd, with all eyes on you expecting you to do something special, speaking into a microphone was much easier. As a matter of fact, on one occasion when on air with Tony, I did comment that it was a lot easier in the comms box. His response was a fairly dry, 'Well you should know.' Perhaps that is why so many sportsmen have turned broadcasters – you can still enjoy the sport, but without all the pressure!

Frustratingly I cannot remember any of my 'pearls' from that match. In fact, I had to look up the result (West Indies won by 47 runs). I do recall that Curtly Ambrose made his international debut but again, time has burnt away the memories of watching a man who went on to take 405 Test wickets. I'm pretty sure that my analysis did not include, 'This guy Ambrose ... I don't think he has what it takes.'

I worked for RJR and other radio stations around the Caribbean up until around the millennium, when my dual radio and television commentary got too much and I had to sacrifice one of them. During some Test matches when combining both roles, I barely had time for lunch and that just would not do!

That first stint with RJR – with Ed, Tony and Reds helping me – was immensely enjoyable and it led to other jobs around the Caribbean. For example, I did commentary for Radio Tempo, a young developing station in Trinidad, which concentrated on regional and cultural events and of course sports, when international matches were staged on the island. This came about with the help of Reds, who convinced Neil Guiseppi, the manager of the station, to include me in their commentary plans. From there I got the opportunity to work for other island stations around the Caribbean.

Back then I looked on my commentary work as something as a subsidy to my main job, which was of course running my gas station in New Kingston. It was some way off from being a viable career option since it was very occasional with our short cricket season. If I was approached, I worked. Essentially I was a freelancer, doing work by the day for around US$100 per day on radio before television came along, but if the Test matches ended early, some stations only paid for as long as the game lasted. The money was okay, but it wasn't something I relied upon and those early finishes cost us commentators!

In 1990, for the first time, cricket was televised out of the

Caribbean to the rest of the world and TWI was accorded the contract for the production with England, the visitors. It was a historic move because previously there had often been just a solitary camera at the ground with the action only shown on the island where the game was taking place, or in a highlights package for the sports news. Apparently part of the TWI deal was that they had to have two local commentators. Tony Cozier was undoubtedly going to be one and he recommended that I be the other. Tony was a big name, the voice of cricket in the Caribbean if you like, having worked for Channel 9, the Australian network, and the BBC.

Those rumblings of nerves that I had first experienced when making a debut as a radio commentator returned for one of my early appearances on television. This time they would affect me – my first words on the box were gibberish. Tony Greig was in the anchor role. He did his opening gambit and then he welcomed me. I said, 'Thanks Tony, and hello to all the ...' I was about to say listeners as my brain automatically went into radio mode, but I managed to stop myself. The problem was the word 'viewers' would not come. I just sat there open-mouthed. It was as if it had fallen out of my brain. After a long pause which to me seemed like an hour but was probably in all reality just a few seconds, I blurted out 'watchers'. As soon as the word had left my lips, I knew I'd made a fool of myself.

You could say there was a bit of symmetry between my first on-screen appearance, my first match for Jamaica and my first Test for West Indies. On all accounts I knew I could improve. Crucially, I knew I would be given the time to get better. Never did I get down or depressed that I had not done myself justice. Perhaps the fact that at the time it never occurred to me that it could be my profession helped.

Not wanting to sound conceited, but I think I have improved. That I have done so has had much to do with John Gayleard, who was the producer for Channel 9's cricket in Australia during those early years and has been a huge influence on my career. John was nicknamed Animal, apparently because his red hair made him look like a cartoon character. I don't know which one and far be it from me to suggest it might have been the Jim Henson muppet of the same name.

Gayleard was in the Caribbean the next year when Australia toured. TWI again was the production company responsible for the pictures, but Channel 9 was responsible for carrying them to the Australian audiences. I again worked on that series and hence again with John, and as the West Indies were touring Australia that same winter of 1991–92, he invited me to Australia to work for Channel 9 during the tour. David Gower was also part of the commentary team because Gayleard did not believe that a commentary team should only consist of people associated with the playing nations. He wanted people he considered good enough to do the job irrespective of where they were from. That outlook was to have an even greater impact on my life, but that comes later.

At Channel 9 I worked with some very experienced and well-respected commentators. Bill Lawry, Richie Benaud and Ian Chappell, for example. I would just sit and listen to those guys while they were on air, trying to pick up as much as possible, Benaud and Chappell in particular because I spent time with them away from the commentary box as well. Benaud had long been considered the master of cricket commentators and Chappell was a man I admired and looked up to. That may come as a surprise bearing in mind our clash in 1976 when he refused to walk, when the whole world except umpire Ledwidge knew he was out caught behind. But I had great respect for him and we have remained eternal friends. At different times all these guys have helped with my development with timely advice.

On one occasion I remember being on commentary with Richie and not saying very much at all. Perhaps his mere presence had intimidated me a bit, but he turned to me and said, 'If you see something that you want to talk about, but it isn't on screen, don't be afraid. You can ask the director for the shot and he'll sort it.' That one bit of advice from the great man made me realise that I could participate more and that he had enough faith in me to try to get me more involved. It was little things like that which instilled the importance of sometimes not just concentrating solely on what was actually being broadcast, but trying to spot something different, something not quite as obvious.

On another occasion when a debatable umpiring decision had been made, I came down heavily on a particular side and said so on air. Richie was more circumspect. At the end of the session, I sought out Ian Chappell, mentioned what had taken place and I asked Ian whether I should not be so outspoken. I wanted to know what was expected of me; after all, I was still learning. 'That's Richie's style,' he said. 'If your style is to be forthright, neither Richie nor anyone will mind.'

Gayleard would move on from Channel 9 to Sky Sports in the UK and we would soon join up again, although not before the BBC made a cheeky bid to sign me to work for them for the West Indies tour to England in the summer of 1995. I was at the gas station when the phone rang. It was a gentleman from the BBC who asked if I would be available to do commentary for the summer. I won't tell you his name because I don't want to cause any embarrassment.

'We were hoping you'd be in England?' he said.

I was irritated. 'You call me at my business and ask me if I'm going to be following the West Indies cricket team around the UK?' I said. 'I don't just pack up and leave my business to follow them everywhere they go, you know.'

'We thought you might be available for some commentary,' he insisted.

'Are you offering me a job or not? An actual position?'

'We'll get back to you,' was his last response.

A letter from the BBC arrived before Christmas in 1994. They were not offering me a job for the duration of the tour. On days when West Indies were playing I would be paid and they would put me up in a hotel, but when they weren't I would have to fund myself and find my own accommodation. By this time I had formed a great relationship with John Gayleard and I called to ask him for advice on whether I should accept the offer. He was in Australia with Sky at the time covering the Ashes tour, which they beamed live back into the UK. Sky did not have rights to show live Tests played in England then, just a highlights package, but showed the overseas tours. He told me not to respond and send him the contract for him to look over.

Early in the new year, Gayleard got back in touch. He made me an offer to work for Sky for the whole summer. They would fly me to England, pay for my board and lodging and pay a salary for the duration of the tour. It was far superior to what the BBC was offering, three times more in fact.

My partnership with Sky had begun and I went back to work for them the following summer, this time not on a contract, but just on days that John could fit me in. It was a much-needed boost to my finances. Melinda, my daughter, wanted to go to university in New York and at the time there was no way I could afford the fees. Gayleard again came to the rescue with offers of work. When Melinda met Gayleard a few years later, I introduced him as 'This is the man who paid for your university.' They both laughed.

It wasn't quite a tug of war for my services between the BBC and Sky. That would come later when Channel 4, Sky and

TWI, who I continued to work with in the Caribbean, wanted me to join them when the principle broadcast rights for England's home Tests became available in 1999.

I was in Dhaka, Bangladesh, covering the ICC Champions Trophy. Gayleard and I were again working together, although this time it was for World Tel, a production company owned by Mark Mascarenhas. Channel 4 were hoping to outbid the BBC for the rights, which they eventually did with ease in a deal worth £103 million to the English Cricket Board, but they needed a production company, which was where TWI thought they could get a slice of the pie.

Somehow they managed to get in touch with me in Dhaka. The telephone lines were hugely unreliable in the city. (The problem always seemed to be at its worst when I tried to call Jamaica.) TWI wanted my signature because they were aware that Channel 4 were interested in me being a part of their commentary team. They probably figured if they pitched to be the production company saying, 'We've got Michael Holding,' it would improve their bargaining position. I listened to TWI's offer, including their offer to fly me to London to meet with Channel 4 when they presented its case.

But there would be no way I would sign a contract with TWI until I heard what Channel 4 had to offer. At this point Sky wasn't involved because Gayleard knew nothing of what was taking place. He only found out when I asked him if it would be possible for me to go to London on one of the off days. I had to explain everything then. It was those telephone lines that were the problem, though. I couldn't get through to Pat Rousseau, my friend and lawyer, to find out what Channel 4's offer was. In turn he couldn't get hold of me. At one time I went as far as to phone a friend in the United States and ask him to call Jamaica to see if there was a problem with the phones there. He called back a few minutes later to say he had got through, no problem. The problem was obviously just getting through from Dhaka.

All this back and forth was taking place over a few days and nothing was being settled. During that tournament, the commentary team and some of the crew used to go by Mark Mascarenhas's suite in the evenings to just hang out and have drinks and sometimes dinner. This particular evening I sought him out for some personal advice. I told him of the developments in England and with TWI and Channel 4. Mascarenhas was not slow with counsel.

He told me: 'If you are signing with a network like Sky or Channel 4, there's a huge difference in terms of monetary value from signing with a production company. I'll use NBC as an example. You would be labelled as an NBC person and you get well rewarded for that.'

He gave me some numbers. They were big ones. So big that I had to sit down immediately. I think I may even have spilt my drink.

'Of course if I was being selfish, I would tell you to sign a contract with me and then I'll sell you to Channel 4,' said a laughing Mascarenhas.

Finally I was able to speak with Pat on the telephone. TWI had confirmed their offer. So had Channel 4. TWI's was inferior. It was less than Channel 4's offer and it was for both the English summer and cricket in the Caribbean. They were trying to get me as cheaply as possible, which I suppose in the business world is only natural, while Mascarenhas was right about the salary on offer from a network.

Not for the first time I went to Gayleard. And not for the first time he told me to do nothing and he would get back to me. Within days he offered me a four-year contract with Sky. The terms were not as good as Channel 4, but there was never any doubt which broadcaster would get my signature. I had to show loyalty. It had to be Sky.

It was an odd feeling being in demand. You have to remember that as a professional cricketer playing in the era in which I did, it was a complete novelty. Never before had organisations pursued me in this way. Okay, county teams Sussex and Lancashire wanted me to sign to play for them at various times, but this was not the same. If it was strange to be wanted, it was wonderful to be able to finally say that broadcasting would be my career. Not to mention that I would not have to worry about finances for a few years. It was a relief, particularly after my fears over my daughter's university fees.

Sadly, one of the guys responsible for securing my future is no longer with us. Mark Mascarenhas was killed in a car crash on his way back from church in Nagpur in early 2002. It was a sad loss as he was at a tender age and he left behind a wife and children. Mark was a very good guy and great company. He really looked after the people who worked for him. He was desperate to make sure everyone was happy and never did he just pay lip service to the idea of a contented workforce. It was one of the reasons he was such a successful businessman. His World Tel company had pulled off a huge coup by winning the broadcast rights for the 1996 World Cup and at the time of his death, he was the agent for Sachin Tendulkar. I will never forget the advice that he gave me while fixing me a drink in Dhaka, nor his spirit of friendship. As you go through life, you encounter people who have a lasting positive influence. Most are mentioned in these memoirs and Mark was one. I raise a glass to him.

14

FROM THE COMMS BOX

Aside from the obvious importance of being able to earn a living, the greatest impact broadcasting has had on my life has been through my relationships. It has allowed me to continue some great friendships and relationships formed during my playing days, I have made many friends, but alas I have also lost friends and supporters. It is an unfortunate trade-off that comes with the job.

Some of the friends I have gained have come from an unlikely source: the players who I used to try to terrorise when I had a ball in my hand. Others are strangers whose living rooms I entered via their television sets. Many have introduced themselves to me to say how much they enjoy my commentary. But sadly, some of those Caribbean supporters who were willing me on to terrorise those batsmen are some of the people who I have lost. That is down to a perception, from a few, that I have somehow been a detractor from West Indies cricket by being honest in the commentary box. It would seem I'm only allowed to say 'good' things about the West Indies team. It is a charge that I find ludicrous but I repeat, it's the view of a minority. It does not worry me, though, as I am a person who prefers to concentrate on the good things in life rather than the bad. It is a source of great joy to me that commentating has allowed me to build friendships and maintain others.

When working on tours in the Caribbean, I am able to meet up with old teammates to reminisce about the good old days, reinforcing bonds that were built years before. When I go around the world I see and work with former opponents and this is where I've had the opportunity to start new friendships with those who were previously on the other side of the fence. Then there are those whose friendship has strengthened since playing days. David Lloyd and Ian 'Beefy' Botham, two great characters, spring to mind. And Ian Chappell, of course.

Chappell took those clashes in the spirit that they were intended. Others less so; they couldn't separate the battle on the field from life off it, but I wouldn't waste ink on them. Another guy who I value like Chappell is the former India Test batsman Aunshuman Gaekwad. I wouldn't have blamed Aunshuman for not wanting to have anything to do with me following the infamous Jamaica Test of 1976. This was the game when Bishan Bedi waved the white flag because he thought the West Indies bowlers were too quick on a wicket that was too inconsistent in bounce and the line of attack too dangerous to endure. I hit Aunshuman, who was as gutsy a batsman as there has ever been, with a nasty blow on the ear during that game and it turned out to be quite a serious injury. It punctured his ear drum and he required an operation. But he never held a grudge and we remain in contact today, sending emails and Christmas cards.

Ravi Shastri is another unlikely friend. Our paths barely crossed as players and the friendship would never have blossomed if it wasn't for commentating. We worked together a lot with Mark Mascarenhas's World Tel production company in places like India, Sharjah and Bangladesh, and discovered we got on well, despite him being about eight years younger. My wife has built a good friendship with his wife, too, and that sort of companionship is invaluable on a tour. I often spend weeks away from home and it is fantastic to know that if I am working with Ravi, that Laurie-Ann can come out too and spend time with Ritu, Ravi's wife. In India a few years ago Laurie-Ann and Ritu took a tour of Rajasthan together and had a great time while the two husbands slaved away in the commentary box.

Another bonus is that I am older, wiser and more appreciative of the different cultures of the countries I visit. As a player you always had to stick to the arrangements made for the team and you could not just go off and see the sights. Now I can. With no practice, training or special duties to perform in between games, I can immerse myself in the culture of the country, something I didn't have the time or perhaps the inclination for when I was younger. It was a lot easier to explore the bright lights at night than the real country during the day.

When I toured India in 1983 and Pakistan in 1980 I hated it. The major cities were fine, but away from the beaten path was torture. Going there with a negative mindset didn't help either. Now when I go back I enjoy both countries. It has been fascinating to see Asia's transformation over the last twenty-odd years.

Today I can use my mobile phone to call anyone in the world. Forgive me if that sounds a little simple, but back in the early 1980s, away from the major cities, trying to make a call was a laborious process. You would have to call the operator in the hotel, who in turn would call the operator in the town. That operator would call a counterpart in Bombay or Karachi, who would then call the operator in London. That operator would then call the Caribbean island. Only then could you get connected. If any of those links were broken, you would have to start again. And it was not an instantaneous process. Usually you would have to book a call before you left the hotel for the ground in the morning and by the time you got back it would be connected – if you were lucky. Those days a comforting call back to family at home was a very precious commodity.

I first went back to Pakistan as a commentator for a series against West Indies in 1997. It was for radio and it was the first time a fully West Indian radio commentary team had broadcast cricket back to the Caribbean. On that tour a lot of West Indies players were complaining about the hotels and food. They had no idea what progress had been made. I kept telling everyone that they should have been around in the Eighties, although to be fair, I spent most of my time then as a player complaining, too. Wes Hall, our manager, told me, 'You've no idea what progress has been made. You should have been here in the Fifties.' It's remarkable how perceptions change over time.

If my hand was forced I would have to say that Australia is my favourite country to tour. Even when playing there I loved it. The weather is always good – okay, Melbourne and Tasmania can be unpredictable, but most of the time you know what you're getting – and the hotels are great. Ian Chappell and Richie Benaud both hail from Down Under, of course, and the great friendship with Ian and a good relationship with Richie are factors that help as a commentator. Nor should the giant Melbourne casino be forgotten as an attraction! England runs Australia a close second. It's the weather that lets the country down, a cliché I know, but like most people from the Caribbean, I am always going to prefer the extreme heat to the extreme cold.

So you see, all these positives of the job far outweigh those negatives of how my relationship with the fans and players has changed.

I have always been very forthright in the commentary box, prepared to call a spade a spade and some of the West Indian fans do not like me being critical of 'their' team. In their opinion, as a former West Indies cricketer, I should be saying only complimentary things about the West Indies team. To that I can only say, I am not a West Indies commentator, I am a commentator from the West Indies.

It has often reached ridiculous proportions. I was accused of having a problem with the whole island of Antigua after doing a radio commentary on Leeward Islands versus Jamaica. Hamish Anthony took quite a few wickets in the game, but his bowling partner Eldine Baptiste was not as successful. I said, 'Anthony has not bowled as well as Baptiste.' The next time I went to Antigua I was accosted and accused of being anti-Antigua because that was where Anthony was from. The huge hole in the argument was that Baptiste was also from Antigua. Antigua is not singular in this attitude. After a few years of doing this job, I have found out that as far as some are concerned, I don't seem to like any island in the Caribbean.

The sad part of it all was that it did not surprise me in the least. Sure, the responses were disappointing, but that is the Caribbean for you. The insularity and island rivalry has been present since time immemorial. Some people in the West Indies only want to hear about the people from their island and woe betide you if they hear something they don't like. Unfortunately it has at times gone beyond childishness. I have been abused in the streets and people have shouted obscenities. Brian Lara, Carl Hooper and Shiv Chanderpaul are some of the players down the years upon whom my views have sparked the most contention. An adverse reaction was guaranteed unless you said only good things about the most popular guys. I remember getting a letter from a man in New York having a pop at me for some comments about Chanderpaul. He wasn't happy. But I used to get worse letters when I was bowling bouncers so it never fazed me.

Only commentators from the West Indies can really under-stand what it is like. Elsewhere in the world you don't seem to get this abuse. For instance, I could be walking to the ground with Tony Greig in Australia and someone would shout something (Greigy was always having digs at the Aussies on Channel 9), but there was always humour, it was only ever done in jest. Never did it have a nasty edge like in the Caribbean. And no one is spared, not even the great legend of Caribbean sports writers and broadcasters that is Tony Cozier.

He cops particularly vociferous stick from Trinidadians if he writes something they don't like about one of their own. In Barbados, too, he has suffered and he is from Barbados. He was accosted and abused when he wrote that Gordon Greenidge should start to think about retiring, never mind he was obviously getting close to the day. Alas, it's typical of the region.

Sometimes the players can react. Since I've begun broadcasting, some have taken such offence that they have refused to speak to me. One West Indies player even brought me up in a team meeting saying, 'Why is he so critical? He used to be one of us.' Can you imagine that? A team meeting of all places.

Once when I was on my way back to the hotel from a match in London, I offered a former player a lift, who asked if I also had room for a particular West Indies player in the taxi. 'Of course,' I said. But when I spun round to collect them, the player refused to get in the taxi and whispered in his pal's ear. He didn't get in, either.

Players take offence wherever you are in the world. They can be very thin-skinned. I've said to so many: 'It's nothing you should worry about, concentrate on your job, don't read the papers and know that if you are doing something wrong your captain or teammates will tell you.' That was my attitude. I never read the newspapers, apart from the *Sporting Life* when I was a player. Again, thankfully the players who take my comments personally are in the minority, just like my playing days with the bouncers.

The majority of players understand why I say what I say.

I still have a lot of friends in the West Indies team because they know that no malice is intended. They know that if I make a mistake I will apologise and they know that I will praise them when it is deserved. Some have listened to me on the radio or television and come to me for advice. Daren Powell, the West Indies fast bowler, and Phil Simmons and Ian Bishop spring to mind immediately and there have been others. I have criticised Daren heavily on air. At Chester-le-Street in 2007 the West Indies were trying to save a game, with himself and Shivnarine Chanderpaul at the crease and he got out to a ridiculous shot. West Indies lost. 'He should've been dropped for that shot,' I said. But Daren knew he had made an error and he didn't take it personally. I coached him when he was starting out as a fast bowler for Jamaica and he still comes to me to talk about his game.

Phil Simmons was opening for West Indies on the 1994 one-day tour of India and had heard that I was tutting away at how he was playing across the line and as a result getting out cheaply. We were in Cuttack and I was doing commentary, high up in this tower that overlooked the ground, when I got a message that Simmons was waiting to see me at the bottom of the steps. If that sounds threatening to you, I can assure you that I felt the same. I didn't know whether he had come along with his cricket bat and was going to hit me across the line or he just wanted a chat. But I went down anyway. 'What can you suggest for my batting problems?' he asked.

Bishop had been having problems with his back in his later days with the West Indies team and I didn't think he was bowling as well as he could, so I said it. In Barbados I think my comment was something like, 'He's not bowling as well as before; he's not the same Ian Bishop.' He came to me for help despite a very close family member's words ringing in his ears, 'What do you want to talk to him for when he can't say anything nice about you.' He was unfortunate; if it hadn't been for his back problems I am sure Bish would have turned out to be an all-time great for the West Indies.

Even my own family have struggled to comprehend my desire to tell it like it is. I have been close friends with Ramnaresh Sarwan for many years and he owns a house only 15 minutes down the road from my home in Miami. He once got out hooking in a Test match in Trinidad, which contributed no end to the West Indies losing the Test and I told the viewers it was a 'brainless' shot. Well, I got it in the neck for that. Not from Ramnaresh but Laurie-Ann, my wife. 'How can you say that?' she shouted at me. 'He's been like a son!' She has always looked upon him as family. I think that proves that I am not in this business to protect friends.

One man who has not been described as my friend is Brian Lara. Some will argue that I have gone out of my way to attack the man, rather than defend him. It is another example of people believing that I am making personal comments instead of calling the action as I see it. People think I don't like Lara because I have often berated him for not putting the team first. It is not true that I don't like him as a person. If I didn't like Lara, I just wouldn't talk to him. I sat down with him in my hotel room for 45 minutes or more in Guyana some years ago after he approached me for a chat about what was going on in his life. If I didn't like Lara and had something personal against the man, he wouldn't have made it past the threshold. The belief that I had some sort of personal vendetta against him got so bad that I went on a radio station in Trinidad to be grilled about it. I knew what was coming, but I went anyway. Question after question was fired at me.

I do not sit behind the mic purely to please people, to only tell them what they want to hear. My job is to tell them how I see it on the field and be objective. I can't colour my comments depending on who's listening. It is their problem, not mine, if they can't spot the difference between someone trying to be objective and a personal attack for other reasons. Sure, commentators will have players that they like and dislike and maybe that creeps into what they say. After all, it is hard to always keep emotions in check. I have been guilty a few times of letting my heart rule my head. I remember when I blew my top in Melbourne on the West Indies' 2000–01 tour. Shane Warne was bowling to a young batsman called Ricardo Powell. He was pretty new to the team. It was a one-day series after the Tests had been completed and throughout the tour there had been some very poor umpiring decisions – a large number of them in favour of Australia. It was the days before we had totally independent umpires so local umpires did all the games. Aussies could officiate an Australia game, Englishmen an England game and so on.

I had a little running battle, if you could call it that, with Bill Lawry over these umpiring decisions. I was keeping a score sheet because I was so disgusted by what I saw as a bias towards the home team. Warne managed to sneak one past Powell's bat to hit him on the pad. He must have been hit on the front foot about nine feet down the pitch from the stumps but Warne, as was his wont, led a huge appeal and the umpire fell for it.

Bill turned to me and joked, 'How many is that now, Mikey?'

I was furious. 'I don't care now, I've lost count,' I said. 'I'm wondering whether he would have been given out if he'd been wearing green and yellow.'

I knew that was a mistake as soon as I said it. Not because I received lots of abuse or people thought I was being unfair, but I felt I had let myself down by allowing my emotions to get to me.

One occasion when I was not worried about speaking my mind on the spur of the moment was in a Test match at

SuperSport Park in South Africa in 2000, which will forever be tagged 'infamous'. It was the game when Hansie Cronje declared to ensure a result against Nasser Hussain's England. Cronje, for reasons we are all now well aware of, was desperate to get Nasser to agree to a chase in the last innings. He was far too keen, kept making proposals which were rebuffed until he went into Godfather mode and made Hussain an offer he couldn't refuse. Of course, Nasser was oblivious to Hansie's motives and he just thought he had been handed a great opportunity for England to win a Test match. The equation involving declarations and the run chase meant that unless it rained again, there was going to be a result that would more likely than not be in England's favour. When this happened, I said, 'If this was in Asia we would all be talking about bookmakers.'

At the time, there was talk of illegal bookies getting involved in games on the Indian subcontinent, but India was the only country mentioned. I suspected that the illegal bookies were trying to influence this game as well, but of course I couldn't be sure. John Gayleard, my old friend, was the producer that day and he was straight in my ear, giving me a telling off. 'What substance have you got to back that comment up?'

I took more stick off air, but would not back down. Sky TV had loads of emails flying in saying that Cronje's decision was great for the game and I was way off the mark with my comments. He had just revived a dead boring game and it was actions like this that would help to create more interest in Test matches. My fellow commentators shared such sentiments. They thought I was talking rubbish, possibly because they were naïve about gambling. They were perhaps unaware of the huge sums of cash that would be put on a draw in a Test match, particularly in Asia. That was why Cronje was so desperate to ensure a result. His accomplices could not stand a draw. My fellow commentators did not grasp that it wasn't about who was going to win or why Cronje was risking losing the Test. It was all about the stalemate. In particular David Gower, who is not a gambler, objected to my assertions. We had an argument about it off air, but he could not see my point.

Next summer when the you-know-what hit the fan and Cronje was exposed, I went on the 'lazy' mic that allows you to talk to the director, who was of course John Gayleard, without it going to air and said, 'Have you anything to say?' He apologised immediately. I then tackled my fellow commentators who were all working that day at Edgbaston. They apologised as well and Gower was quick to leave the studio where he was to come over, say sorry and chat things over. He is a pretty unflappable guy and would never shoot from the hip like I would. That is what it is like in the commentary box. Much like a dressing room, you have different personalities and what will work for one person will be alien to another.

Two people I have worked with who are poles apart are Bill Lawry and Ian Botham. Bill has an eye for detail and makes sure he is 100 per cent prepared for a day's commentating while Beefy is ... well Beefy. At the start of the day's play, Bill is the first on the microphone for Channel 9 because he can be quite excitable and the network thinks that he can grab the audience, pulling the viewers along with him on this rollercoaster ride. He is in his seat for about 45 minutes before the first ball is bowled, checking everything is working okay and ensuring he has cards with stats on laid out in front of him. He is completely prepared, just as he was as a batsman. He left nothing to chance then and was meticulous in his approach. He is exactly the same as a commentator.

Beefy is none of the above. He will get to the ground as late as the producer will allow him to. If he is doing his pitch report he just walks straight out there, has a look and is then ready to go to camera. He is not one for preparatory work, shall we say, but that does not make him any less of a commentator. The feedback from Sky viewers will attest to that.

The commentator that I have to field most questions about when I am out and about is dear old David 'Bumble' Lloyd. 'Is he as bonkers as he comes across?' I'm asked.

'Absolutely,' I tell them without hesitation.

Bumble can be serious when he needs to be, although most of the time he is having fun. He can get away with saying things that others cannot. In Australia for the last Ashes tour, he was on particularly good form. He had an oyster fetish on that tour and for some reason he decided to try to eat a thousand of them over the duration of the tour. (Don't ask me why.) During commentary someone asked him how his oyster opus was going: 'How many are you up to now?' Bumble, with a cheeky look on his face, quipped: 'It puts lead in your pencil, you know!'

There was pandemonium in the box when he said that. His co-commentator couldn't speak for the laughter, the rest of us were in a terrible state and Barney Francis, the poor producer, could only manage a feint 'Bumble, please' because it was suppressed by snorts. He had an unforgettable look of fear in his eye. He knew there would be more.

Bumble, knowing he had his audience and a co-commentator silenced, delivered the pay off: 'But with all that lead in your pencil, it's very important to have someone to write to.'

15

LOVE OF THE HORSES

I must have been aged six or seven when my love affair with horses and horseracing began. Early one morning I was raised from my slumber by my brother, Ralph, to help cut some grass from a patch of land at the back of our home on Dunrobin Avenue for his godmother and our neighbour, Nurse Skeffrey. I was always one who enjoyed my sleep so, looking back, I can't have been that happy about it, but I wanted to be with my brother when he went on his escapades so did what was required.

Nurse Skeffrey owned a few horses and once the grass was boxed, we got into the car for a 40-minute drive to Caymanas Park racetrack to deliver it to the beasts. Not that I was awake when we got there that first morning. I had drifted back to sleep and when I awoke, I rubbed my eyes in disbelief. The sight of these powerful, athletic animals fascinated me. I had caught the bug.

Horseracing and cricket have always been my chief passions and they have both enriched my life no end. Luckily my successful cricket career has allowed me to own horses, try my hand at breeding them and form a close friendship with the legendary trainer, Sir Michael Stoute. My brief venture into owning and breeding took place in Jamaica, where it was much easier and cheaper to get involved. I am so absorbed by the sport that when I was offered work in the UK by Sky on the

Windies tour of 1995 and asked where I wanted to be based, without hesitation I said Newmarket. You see on that first venture with Sky, they were paying my expenses, which included rented accommodation for the tour. Fortunately, the person asking the question was John Gayleard, the cricket producer at Sky, who knew me very well and apart from that, accommodation in Newmarket was certainly a lot cheaper than anything in London where the Sky offices are based. There were no objections and with my past connections, and with the help of one particular good friend in Janet Anderson, who previously worked in Sir Michael's office, each year very comfortable abodes were always found until I bought my own house. These days with my continued association with Sky, I spend almost half of my year at my home in the Cambridgeshire town of Newmarket, the epicentre of British racing. The other half is spent in Miami and Jamaica, unless I'm travelling for work in other far-flung lands. If I'm not in Newmarket, I am always logging onto the internet to check on the form of horses and listening to internet racing radio for the latest news.

Every time I enter Sir Michael's racing stables, I still get the same buzz as I did as a youngster on that first trip to Caymanas Park. The brute force these animals have seems to contradict their manner. They have wonderful personalities, and although there are some horses who you don't want to get too close to, most you can go up to and give them a pat and a stroke. If I am honest though, it's the speed I love most. It is very special. It is a weakness of mine, I suppose! From fast bowling to fast cars – I love it. There are few more graceful sights than a thoroughbred at full tilt, nostrils flared with muscles bulging as the body strives for the line.

The horseracing and cricket communities have always mixed well, too. Sir Garfield Sobers, Wes Hall (who would believe

the great big fast bowler had a son who became a jockey?),
Richie Benaud and Mike Atherton, to name but a few, have
loved their horses. Likewise lots of horseracing people love
cricket.

From those early days at Caymanas Park, doing my little bit
to help Nurse Skeffrey look after her horses, I progressed to
being a keen student of the game, studying the form of trainers,
jockeys and horses. Perhaps I should have been concentrating
on my studies at Kingston College, but two friends of mine
made sure my interest never wavered. They were always debat-
ing which of the two Jamaica trainers, Billy Williams or Laurie
Silvera, were the best during their glory days of the 1960s and
early '70s. And of course there was much discussion about their
stable jockeys, Kenneth Mattis and Winston Ellis. I didn't want
to feel left out so I started to do my homework and added my
two bits every now and again.

Inevitably when one takes such a deep interest in horseracing,
one's eye is caught by the odds offered by the bookmakers.
Now, no gambler ever admits to how much they really stake,
and given I was at school at the time, I am not about to break
that rule so let's just say I had only a few pennies on each-way
chances. In those days, however, pennies could keep you fed
for the entire day and it wasn't uncommon for me and my clan
of racing friends to not quite make it to the canteen on some
school days. No cash, no lunch.

I soon started taking note of what was happening in England,
hearing about the great partnerships like Joe Mercer and Peter
Walwyn, Geoff Lewis and Noel Murless. Later on when I went
to the country as a player, I got to appreciate such fine jockeys
as Willie Carson and Pat Eddery in person. Closer association
with some of the jockeys in England came later after meeting
Sir Michael. Such names like Greville Starkey and the great
Lester Piggott, who we in Jamaica only read about and

marvelled at their brilliance, became people I actually met. Then there was Walter Swinburn, Sir Michael's stable jockey when I first met him. Walter was a superb rider. In a race he was always in the right position on a horse and if he lost, it would almost never be because of a mistake he had made, rather just the simple fact that the horse wasn't good enough on the day.

I remember watching these guys in action on the track and being in awe at their talent. I was a fan in the same way that spectators would revere other sportsmen like footballers, cricketers or golfers. And when I came to meet these people I would be star-struck. I was like this when I first met Sir Michael. I was introduced to Stoutie by Ronald Burke, a Barbados trainer. Ronald had been married to Susan, the daughter of Nigel Nunes, the gentleman who trained my horses in Jamaica at the time. He knew Stoutie and when he was in Newmarket in 1985, he got in touch and asked if I wanted to come down to meet the great man. I was playing for Derbyshire at the time. He need not have asked, all I needed was directions and I was down there on my first day off.

I've been going back every year since. When I was with Derbyshire and had time off, or if I was just passing through the UK, I made sure the stopover was for a day or two and would go to stay with Jimmy and Shirley Scott. Jimmy was Stoutie's travelling head lad and I became good friends with them. As I've mentioned, when I signed my first long-term contract with Sky, I rented a place in Newmarket in 1999 and finally bought a house six years later, a modern place near the hospital.

Through the association with Jimmy and Shirley, my friendship with Stoutie grew. In the early days I would just go to the yard and whenever possible watch them work on the heath. Then occasionally I would travel with Jimmy in the horse box to the races, then it progressed to me being invited over to the house for breakfast. Now I would go because he expects me to. What the heck, it's been more than 20 years.

To this day I remain in awe of Stoutie and am careful not to get in his way or pester him with too many questions or opinions about horses. What helps our relationship is that Stoutie is a huge cricket fan. He was born in Barbados so supports West Indies and loves to see them do well, but more important for him is seeing good cricket played. He is a purist. Of the modern era, players like Alec Stewart and Mike Atherton were his favourites because they were what he called 'proper batsmen', ones who knew the value of their wicket. He is not a fan of those guys who go out and play a few flashy shots and then throw it away.

He loves to talk cricket because I guess it takes his mind off the stress of training. Given the opportunity, he can talk about the game for hours and the horses take a back seat for a while. Indeed, if I'm away on tour, he will phone me up to talk about cricket or a match which is going on.

It was thanks partly to cricket that he got his knighthood, and before anyone starts wondering, it wasn't his playing. Every year he would take cricket teams, made up of horseracing enthusiasts, to Barbados for a tour and because he introduced people to the island who invested in property and business, the government recommended he be knighted. He contributed a great deal to the Barbados tourist economy and the government appreciated it.

I consider it a great honour to be called a friend and in that regard I hope that when I'm around, I'm able to relieve some of the pressure he is under, which can be tremendous in Flat racing. He is in charge of horses whose owners have paid huge sums of money for them and much is expected, not to mention the high standards and expectancy he sets for himself.

Sometimes, while walking around the yard, he will have a very serious look on his face and you know he is thinking deeply and you don't want to disturb him. He can be very intense at times, but if you get him away from it all he is like a kid. Over dinner, horses will not come up in conversation at all and he will be himself, his Caribbean heritage will come out and he will be incredibly laid-back.

Likewise if you get him out on the cricket field. Stoutie is an okay cricketer and, to be polite, his love for the game is greater than his skill, but of course this is true of most who don't make a living from the game and only play recreationally. He plays for the Newmarket XI as a batsman, although his appearances are becoming fewer. He has a few good shots and I'll admit that his cover drive is not too shabby. I used to join him and other famous horseracing names like Julian Wilson, William Haggas and Ed Dunlop in the Newmarket XI in the early days when I still found it fun to get involved. My last game was against the Royal Household at Frogmore on the grounds of Windsor Castle in 2003, after being dragged out of retirement. Thankfully, Stoutie has never asked me for tips on how to improve his run-making ability because I have never been known to beat around the bush! But I am quite happy to discuss the game with him.

I must admit that I got a huge buzz in the summer of 2008 when Stoutie said something very special about me during an interview with the BBC's Rishi Persad. Rishi had come up to the yard to do a piece about Stoutie and his Derby entrants and he interviewed me for a bit, because I was always around, and then spoke with Stoutie. When I saw it on television a few days later, I was stunned. 'Mikey is a part of the team,' said Stoutie. Well, when I heard that I felt terrific. It lifted me no end. Here was one of the greatest trainers ever saying I was helping him out, a part of his team.

Now, I might help to move a horse pen every now and again, carry a bucket of food to the stable door once in 24 years, or give the lads and lasses a leg up, but that is about it. Most of the time I am just observing; on the heath from six in the morning, or listening to the chatter over breakfast, or just mixing with the lads and lasses in the yard.

People have asked me what I think of Stoutie as a trainer. I tell them that the figures are there for all to see. He has been training winners of the biggest races since 1978 and was the only twentieth-century trainer to win a Classic in five successive seasons. What people don't see, however, is how Stoutie is around the yard or on the gallops. It is a privilege to see and having enjoyed watching him at work for many years, I have come to the conclusion that he is a genius.

The guy must have an incredible memory. I have come to believe that it must be photographic and this opinion is reinforced when I watch him writing imaginary notes in the middle of his palm with his imaginary pen. I think that's how he imprints things in his brain and believe it or not, sometimes he writes his imaginary notes and then rubs them out as if he doesn't want anyone to see them! Only very rarely will you see him studying the real notes about a horse; as they walk past him in the morning he will know exactly what each of them has done – he won't have a piece of paper to tell him. And he'll just shout out the instructions to the jockeys as they pass. Sometimes he will stop one of them, have a think and then it will come to him what this particular horse needs to be doing. Then the instructions will be issued again. I look on in wonder at how he can remember it all. It would be hard enough for a trainer who has 20 horses, but Stoutie has up to two hundred.

Only on what are called 'work mornings', when most of the horses do serious fast work, will he always have his 'work sheet'. When watching him work with the horses, it can pay to stay quiet because he will make certain comments that make your ears prick up. Nothing like, 'Hey, have a bet on this', but maybe, 'That horse has improved for the run.' When he utters these words, you know that this is a horse to watch.

One year he had five fillies out that were all being prepared for Classic races. We had just had a particularly bad spring and the ground was very soft. One of these horses had not enjoyed the ground at all and had really backed off in its work. On a late morning in June, this filly was out again to do fast work and Stoutie narrowed his gaze as he studied it working past him. He smiled and rubbed his hands together as an unrecognisable sound came from from his lips. It was almost like someone blowing into a musical instrument, only not so musical. It is a famous thing he does when he sees something he likes. 'She's only rated 82 you know, Mikey,' was the comment as he rode off on his hack to meet the horses at the top of the gallop. Next time that horse ran, it was a handicap at Haydock Park and I had my biggest-ever bet. No need to say what happened; gamblers don't talk too much about losing bets.

Prior to this I had backed his horses religiously because I was unable to separate my emotions from facts and figures. I wanted them to win so I would bet on them. As a punter this was a recipe for disaster, but as time has gone on I have been able to put my feelings to one side. I still want them to win, but when all good sense says they won't, I keep my money in my pocket. And as I've been able to spend more and more time with the horses when watching them at work, I have formed my own opinions and I might mutter to myself such thing as 'That ain't so good' or 'Mediocre – ain't never going to back that'. Or more times than not, 'One to keep tabs on'. Backing winners always gives you a great feeling, but backing one of Stoutie's winners is even more pleasurable, especially if it's a meaningful race.

One of Stoutie's horses that I backed recently was Conduit

in its Breeders' Cup Turf triumph at Santa Anita in 2008. Laurie-Ann and I made the trip over to California. Laurie-Ann had a marathon to run in San Diego on the Sunday and I thought it was an ideal opportunity to fit the Breeders' Cup meeting in on the Friday and Saturday. Before the race, my palms were sweating and my heart was thumping in my chest. I was oblivious to the people around me. During the race, I was shouting and screaming and the Americans, who were all cheering on their own hotly fancied horses, soon became very quiet as Conduit stormed to victory. With all the noise I was making, they must have thought, 'Who is this guy?' It is a great feeling to see a horse win a big race like that when you have followed its progress in the yard, much like the lift you get when a horse you own wins a race.

I have owned a few in my time, although to put the record straight, not the one named Whispering Death. It was pure coincidence that it was named after me. I just happened to phone the trainer, William Haggas, when he was with its owners when they were discussing what they should call it.

'It's Mikey, I've got to take this call,' he said. After he hung up they asked him: 'Which Mikey was that?' So Whispering Death it was.

My racehorse-owning days were in Jamaica, but I got out of the game in 1998 because I was spending too much time away from home and there was no point in owning horses and not being around to see them run. However, I got great pleasure from it, memorably from my first horse called Undercover.

Trainer Nigel Nunes had Undercover, which had not been picked up from a stud farm sale, and it was available to buy. I never had the sort of money being asked for so he asked if I wanted to lease it. I went to Howard Hamilton, the friend I had met years before when he was working with Shell when they sponsored the domestic competition in West Indies, and suggested sharing the training fees with him. These were the only expenses that we accrued under the deal and we got to pocket any prize money won. At the end of Undercover's racing days, it went back to the original owners for breeding purposes.

Undercover was far from top class, but still managed to win quite a few little races. We had a system in Jamaica where the best horses were ranked 'A1', and then the rest would follow A2, B1, B2 and so on. Undercover made it to A2, but didn't win any races in that section.

Early in her racing career, in a prep race for a classic, she went off at 99–1 so it would be fair to say that Howard and I did not have high hopes that afternoon. Surprisingly, she led the field for the whole race until the last furlong and finished fourth. After the race, Howard, in an excitable state, went out onto the track to lead Undercover in because he was so proud. Howard has owned and continues to own many outstanding horses in Jamaica, but he couldn't believe the race Undercover had run. When he was leading our steed back in, he was looking at her as if to say, 'How have you done that? You don't have the ability.'

Undercover spoilt me because when your first horse does so well, you think the racing game is easy. It's not. It is a tough, tough business. One of my horses fractured a knee in its first-ever race and never raced again. That can be heartbreaking, but others, like Precocious and Bunny's Halo, won one race and a handful respectively.

Overall I have to say I've been very lucky with my horse ownership exploits in Jamaica. Not so much so in the UK, however. Walter Swinburn and I formed a great friendship and when he took over from his father-in-law Peter Harris and started training, I got involved in two syndicates at his stables. Neither venture has proved fruitful, but there is still time and as it's a lot less expense than actually purchasing a horse, who knows what might come of it?

It is difficult to explain the buzz you get from watching a horse you own race. You just feel on top of the world when your horse wins. It is an adrenalin rush that I never experienced in cricket. It is probably superior to taking a wicket in a Test match because the feeling lasts so much longer. If I worked out a plan for a batsman and it came off, or if I dismissed a particularly dangerous batsman, I would be elated, but I would have to come down again from that high to an even keel to concentrate on the next ball. After your horse has won, the feeling doesn't leave you. It will be with you when you leave the course and when you're having supper that evening. It will still be there when you wake up in the morning. Fast bowling didn't do that.

A recent highlight arising from my horse passion was when I was invited to take part in the Royal procession at Royal Ascot in 2009. I was forewarned that someone who worked for the Queen would be calling me to ask if I would like to attend, which was just as well as I would have reckoned it was a wind-up. Anyway, Laurie-Ann and I went, with me in my hired top hat and tails (I'd never had call for such attire before!), to have lunch with Her Majesty at Windsor Castle before joining the procession in the carriages for that famous ride down the Ascot straight, then spent the day in the Royal Box. It was a real honour and something that I'm unlikely to experience again. I was, of course, on my best behaviour and even if the Queen and I did have a chat about cricket, I think it would be right if I kept to myself what she said.

16

MR STANFORD

Appearances can be deceptive. To the world, Sir Allen Stanford would have looked like a chubby-cheeked and jovial benefactor ready to bankroll West Indies cricket as he revelled in his 'Stanford Twenty20 for $20m' one-off cricket match. Like any good politician, with cameraman in tow he constantly toured the ground he had built, kissed babies, bounced pretty ladies on his knee and mingled with players in the dressing rooms.

But from my experience, the real Sir Allen was somewhat different. That big, wide smile could disappear in an instant, making way for a temper that scared his employees and even put me on edge a few times. And as for being the self-proclaimed saviour of West Indies cricket, well, just as I thought, this has been proven to be more than debatable.

Over five years, as he set up the West Indies Cricket Hall of Fame at his Sticky Wicket restaurant at the Stanford cricket ground in Antigua, a domestic Twenty20 competition for the Caribbean and the now infamous '$20m' Stanford Super Series, Sir Allen consistently declared that he was spending money in the interests of the game in the Caribbean. I begged to differ.

Throughout this chapter I will give you examples of why I believe Sir Allen only got involved in Caribbean cricket because he wanted to boost his own ego, his own companies and, eventually, his own bank balance. I will assert that West Indies Cricket Board (WICB) was forced by Sir Allen to sign a contract giving up its right to be paid $3.5m for its part in the 'Stanford Twenty20 for $20m'. In the end the competition was more like 'Twenty20 for $16.5m' – the England and Wales Cricket Board (ECB) got its $3.5m, but not the WICB.

That 'cheap' shot confirmed what I had already known. How can you propose to be helping West Indies Cricket and then do such a thing? The main reason I ended my association with the man was because of the way he consistently tried to fool the public by proclaiming every chance he got that he was going to take West Indies back to the top of the world game when I don't believe that was his primary purpose at all. If he had been more frank from the start, and I had known what I later found out after joining the board and gotten closer to his inner workings, I would never have become involved and I would never have had issues with him. After all, it's his money and he has the right to spend it as he feels, or so we all thought at the time. The revelations have shown that it's debatable whether the funds were really even his.

Despite my disagreement with Sir Allen, I concede that he has done some good for the game. The Stanford ground he built in Coolidge is a lovely facility and the domestic Twenty20 competition has at least revived some interest in, and possibly attracted some new audiences to, cricket in the West Indies. Still, that winning smile, gregarious personality and dollar signs that people saw when Sir Allen first became involved in our game has done more harm than good, causing division and further weakening a West Indies Cricket Board just when it needed to be strong. But as I've said, appearances can be deceptive.

The first time I met Sir Allen was in May 2003 when he had set up the Hall of Fame for West Indies Cricket, something which had never been done before; surprising really, considering the tradition of cricket in the region. Sir Everton Weekes,

Sir Vivian Richards, Sir Garfield Sobers, George Headley, Malcolm Marshall, Clive Lloyd, Lance Gibbs, Andy Roberts, Courtney Walsh, Curtly Ambrose, Brian Lara and myself were to be honoured. We were the first inductees so it was very special, and there was much pomp and ceremony at the Sticky Wicket restaurant – a sort of cricket-themed sports bar – at Sir Allen's own cricket ground in Coolidge, Antigua. There were cricket pictures on the wall, and at the front of the restaurant there were busts of us all, with a small biography and above, the flag of our respective countries fluttering in the breeze.

He welcomed us warmly and we reciprocated. Obviously it was a privilege for me to be named with those great players in such a way and I thought that Sir Allen's efforts to recognise cricket by doing this were to be applauded. Other than this event, I had little else to do with him – he was someone who I knew had plenty of money and I thought he was just a businessman who loved cricket. After all, I had come across plenty of similar people during my career touring the world.

To give you a brief biography, Sir Allen hailed from Houston, Texas, and had made much of his fortune in real estate in his home city before moving into global wealth management. From here on things get a bit murky. The Stanford Financial Group, of which he was chairman, had assets worth more than $50 billion, while Forbes listed him as America's 205th richest American in 2008. He moved to the US Virgin Islands from Antigua where he had been living and had become a citizen of Antigua and Barbuda in the late 1990s, which, I presume, is when his interest in cricket began.

I did not think our paths would cross again after that induction ceremony. It would be another two years before I met him again. By 2005 Laurie-Ann and her friend, Rhonda Kelly, had set up a sponsorship and event management company called KellyHolding Ltd. Laurie-Ann had good experience of cricket in the West Indies because she had worked for the WICB previously and her friend Rhonda had worked for the previous sponsors of West Indies cricket, Cable and Wireless, in their regional sponsorship department, so it was no surprise with their background that the company was employed by Digicel, who were the new sponsors of the West Indies team, to manage their home series.

That year South Africa were in the Caribbean and when the two sides got to Antigua for the fourth and final Test at the end of April, Laurie-Ann, who is from Antigua and wanted to do something special, acted on an idea put forward by Richard Nowell from Digicel and decided that the Digicel function this time around should be a fun game of cricket at Sir Allen's ground, instead of the obligatory cocktail party that players can get tired of.

Both teams attended but did not take part in the match. Instead former players, including Sir Viv Richards, and other former first-class cricketers, sprinkled with the odd celebrity, provided the action on the pitch while the West Indian and South African cricketers watched from the boundary, relaxing and having fun. Some of them shared the task of umpiring and Makhaya Ntini, the South Africa fast bowler, toured the ground mingling and partying with spectators, who were not charged for entrance. There was a great vibe about the event, which was held at night under the lights. Richie Richardson and Curtly Ambrose brought their band, Big Bad Dread and the Baldhead, to play a mix of reggae and some singalong originals. I must say that I think Richie and Curtly were better cricketers than they are musicians, but their band was still very good!

Apparently Sir Allen had been at the ground throughout and had seen that the event was a great success and heard that Laurie-Ann's company had organised it, so he invited us to have dinner with him at another of his restaurants, The Pavilion, set atop a hill which overlooked the Stanford ground. I think the carnival atmosphere at the match might have triggered something in his mind. After all, when the Stanford Twenty20 domestic competition matches took place at the ground, they were very similar in terms of atmosphere, with lots of music and people generally having a good time. When the dinner invitation was extended, I was caught totally by surprise and had no idea why he wanted to meet with us. This is a restaurant that requires a code of dress of at least a jacket, if not a suit. I had neither in Antigua. I was only there as part of the television commentary team and that sort of finery was never required for work in the Caribbean. Fortunately we got there early and the manager of the establishment lent me a jacket that they apparently kept for people in my situation – problem solved.

During the meal Sir Allen told us that he wanted to help West Indies cricket get back to the glory days of the past. Well, this was exactly what I wanted to hear. Someone with his financial clout could make a real difference to the structure of the game and following his Hall of Fame idea, I felt it was clear that his love for the game was genuine. Laurie-Ann was excited, too, because West Indies cricket was also close to her heart.

Then he mentioned his idea for a Twenty20 competition, saying that he wanted something fast-paced and fun like what he had seen at the Digicel function. My heart sank. What had taken place that night was what it was: for fun and to get rid of the monotony of the cocktail parties that the cricketers face on tours. It could never be thought of as a development process.

'You've lost me Mr Stanford,' I said. (He was just a humble Mr then; he was not knighted until November 2006.)

I told him that West Indies cricket needed something more substantial than a Twenty20 tournament to become a world force again. I felt it was too far removed from Test cricket, the format of the game that a country was judged on, to make a meaningful impact. Nor did I like Twenty20 for the way it 'dumbed down' our wonderful game.

His response was that the shorter form of the game was the way he had to go as he wanted every island in the region to be represented. The tournament would be too long otherwise. What he said obviously made sense if every island had a team, but I couldn't see Twenty20 cricket doing what he had proposed: to get West Indies cricket back to the top. I told him I would not be a part of it.

Sir Allen still wanted KellyHolding to organise the logistics of the whole tournament. After consulting her partner later on, Laurie-Ann agreed. However, at the first meeting to discuss the logistics of the 2006 Stanford Twenty20, which would see 19 teams take part, he asked her, 'Where's Mikey?'

It was surprising that he had asked because I thought I had made it clear during our dinner that I would not be involved in helping to set up the tournament. I reasoned that it was an example of him being used to getting what he wanted. Laurie-Ann soon let him know that I had meant what I had said at the dinner.

Stanford wanted to develop a board of 'Legends' and 14 former players were recommended to him by Laurie-Ann and Rhonda: Clive Lloyd, Lance Gibbs, Ian Bishop, Sir Everton Weekes, Desmond Haynes, Courtney Walsh, Sir Viv Richards, Sir Garfield Sobers, Gordon Greenidge, Joel Garner, Wes Hall, Richie Richardson, Curtly Ambrose and Andy Roberts were asked and they all accepted the invitation to join the Stanford board. As well as helping put the cricketing logistics in place, like rules and regulations, it was the roll of the Legends to visit teams to offer advice on coaching or preparation for matches. They were like the liaison officers between the Stanford

Twenty20 organisation and the island boards. For this they were paid US$10,000 a month.

When the plans were announced for the Stanford Twenty20, it was clear that Sir Allen was pumping in a lot of money. The initial investment was $28 million, but nearly half of that was for a match planned that year between a team comprising the best players from that inaugural tournament and an international side. That game didn't happen in the first year because of scheduling problems, but the idea eventually re-emerged as the 'Twenty20 for $20m' challenge match.

The 2006 tournament was a success and generated a great deal of interest around the region with its US$1 million winner's prize money, $500,000 for the runner up, and $200,000 and $100,000 going to the winners and runners-up cricket associations. There were also healthy Man of the Match and Play of the Match prizes allocated for each game. This wasn't all the money available either. Each island represented at the tournament saw their cricket boards given $280,000 in the first year to help with their infrastructure, training and general preparation of the teams for the tournament, with $180,000 per year, or $15,000 per month, promised thereafter. The money was a godsend for the boards, which included the Barbados Cricket Association, Guyana Cricket Board, Jamaica Cricket Association, Trinidad & Tobago Cricket Board and the smaller islands that fell under the Leeward and Windward Islands Cricket Association. Each got the same amount. Other islands that fell outside of the purview of the WICB like Cayman, US Virgin, the Bahamas and British Virgin also got their share.

Not long after that first tournament, Sir Allen decided to spend even more money on his project. Early in 2007 he began setting up a professional team in Antigua. He was living there at the time and of course his ground and facilities were readily available. The Antigua team was meant to be the model around which further pro-teams were to be formed at a later date. Sir Allen then got a bit anxious about putting other pro-teams in place and three more islands were added to the project, namely Anguilla, Nevis and St. Lucia. This meant players would be paid to play and not have to worry about finding other jobs. Money would be spent on training facilities, coaches and physiotherapists. West Indies cricket would obviously benefit from such investment and although I doubted that Twenty20 could produce Test players, it had to be a good thing that there were professional cricketers across the islands who were improving and developing, thanks to this money and the opportunity to now concentrate solely on cricket.

There wasn't a tournament in 2007 because the packed schedule of both domestic and international cricket committed to by the WICB left no window of opportunity apart from the summer months. Sir Allen did not want to have it in the summer, so another was scheduled for the following year.

In 2007 I was due back in Antigua to see more players inducted into the Hall of Fame at the Sticky Wicket. Two men I knew very well, Reverend Wes Hall and the late Sir Clyde Walcott, were to be honoured. Wes was a very good friend and Clyde had been team manager when I was playing, proving to be approachable and understanding. I had been asked to say a few words about both at the ceremony.

There was a dinner at the Pavilion restaurant afterwards, during which Sir Allen was very vocal in telling people that I would not be one of his Legends, implying that I was being unsupportive. This irritated me. The next day I went to speak to him because I wanted to set the record straight. With the money the islands were getting, I would have to be a very stubborn man indeed not to recognise that it was a good thing. Some of my comms box associates and friends will laugh when reading the previous sentence with reference to my stubbornness, but although I will admit to this trait, I would have to be both stubborn *and* foolish to not recognise all this funding had to do some good. I told Sir Allen that it was wrong to say that I was not behind what he was trying to do and how pleased I was that West Indies would benefit.

'Why not join the Legends then?' he asked.

'I don't need to be on the Board to be supportive,' I said. 'And with all the travelling I do, I would rarely make the meetings or be able to fulfil any other commitments.'

'There are fax machines, emails and teleconferencing facilities, Mikey. I want you on the board.'

'I'll think about it,' I told him.

I was still unsure, so I called Pat Rousseau, my friend, lawyer, advisor and a former WICB president for advice. You see, Stanford wasn't seen as our saviour in every quarter in the Caribbean. In fact there had been rumblings from some that he was using The Legends and their good names to give himself credibility. Pat told me: 'Mikey, there's no problem with you joining the Board, but if there is anything you are unhappy or uncomfortable about you must speak up and if nothing changes after you've spoken, you'll have to resign.'

The next day I told Sir Allen I would be happy to join the Board. Initially I was invited to a board meeting as a guest. It was proposed that I join and I was then asked to leave the room while a vote was taken. No objections were made, so in May 2007, I became a Stanford Legend and board member.

Not that I would last very long – ten months in fact. After agreeing to become a Legend, I immediately had to leave for England for commentary duty for Sky Sports, so I did not actually attend a board meeting until October. I was there for the November meeting, there wasn't one in December because of Christmas, and I was in my seat for the January meeting, although I was soon shifting uncomfortably. It would be my last.

As I mentioned earlier, all of the Legends had been acting as a sort of liaison between the teams and the Stanford organisation. In fact the Legends had all been assigned an island to visit a couple of times a month to check on progress and help out. Desmond Haynes, the former West Indies batsman, and I visited the US Virgin Islands. We went to practice sessions, gave advice on the development of players and, because the board there did not have a proper constitution, we set the wheels in motion to get one sorted out. It was satisfying work.

However, when some of the Legends toured the islands and returned to discuss issues, there was a feeling that some of the money the islands had received was not being spent in the correct way. Dessie and I certainly had a sort of sixth sense that money was not going to the people that it should and spoke to Sir Allen's auditor about putting checks in place to ensure the money was spent in the correct way. So when I learnt that the funding for islands was on the agenda for the January meeting, I assumed that we would be talking about this issue.

This meeting took place at the Sticky Wicket restaurant. On the top floor towards the back there was a room with tables shaped in a huge U. Sir Allen sat at the top of the bend with his girlfriend Andrea Stoelker, who had been appointed President of the Stanford Twenty20 board, one of his lawyers who was also a board member, along with Laurie-Ann and Rhonda among one or two others. The rest of us, the Legends, would spread out on the arms. He was the centre of attention, as he was entitled to be.

Understandably Sir Allen was frustrated by the way some of the money was being wasted. But I did not expect him to make such a forceful case for it to be stopped completely. He was not intimidating, nor did he raise his voice, but he made sure that everyone knew that this was his money and he thought he was being taken advantage of.

I remembered the advice from Pat Rousseau. I had to speak up because stopping the funding was a ludicrous idea, just a knee-jerk reaction to a problem which could easily be solved. I argued strongly it should not be stopped, gave examples of the ways and means money *was* being spent correctly, but it seemed to fall mostly on deaf ears. In fact, most of the Legends just sat there and didn't say anything, an attitude I couldn't understand. Only Wes Hall and possibly one or two others agreed with me and said it shouldn't be stopped. We were being paid good money and I certainly didn't want to be there cashing pay cheques without trying to make a difference, getting involved in discussions and making decisions. The discussions continued, but soon the resistance to Sir Allen's wishes diminished; I think the phrase is 'the silence was deafening'. It was obvious that Sir Allen wanted to stop the funding and I suppose the few supporting my view or who thought otherwise felt it was fruitless to continue arguing.

Eventually it went to the vote with the motion: should funding be cut? There was only one vote that was not a 'yes'. It was mine. I had been completely out-voted. I was angry and felt let down.

After the meeting those of us who were not from Antigua were in the minibus, waiting to be taken back to the Tradewinds Hotel, where we stayed each time we visited for a meeting. I sat in the front, contemplating my future with the Board although I already knew what I had to do.

One board member at the back of the bus piped up: 'Mikey had a point back there.' I was flabbergasted because this person was one who seemed to have his lips sewn together in the meeting. 'Why didn't you say that, then?' I asked.

More of them started to chime in. 'Yeah, those were good

ideas, Mikey.' Well, I lost my cool right there and then, raising my voice.

'Well, it's too late now. The vote has been taken,' I shouted. 'Why didn't you speak up?' For the rest of the journey back to the hotel I quietly seethed, barely able to comprehend why so many of my fellow board members had not supported these 'good ideas' that I had suggested. I don't know why they did it and I don't want to second guess their reasons. I am only relating the facts as I know them. However, there were a lot of big names on that board and there was a certain irony that these great West Indies players had voted to stop funding which could have helped to produce future greats.

As for me, I had come to the conclusion that I had to resign from the Board. It was clear that Sir Allen had no interest in furthering cricket in the Caribbean if he was prepared to stop funding. It made a mockery of his claims that he wanted to do the best for West Indies cricket. When I flew back home from Antigua, I wrote my resignation letter, showed it to Pat Rousseau for him to check over and then sent it on to Sir Allen.

10th January 2008

Dear Sir Allen

It is with great regret that I am writing this letter to you, offering my resignation from the Stanford Twenty20 board as of February 25th, the last scheduled day of the 2008 tournament. As you are well aware, my reason for joining the board was closely linked to the fact that your initiative was going beyond just the Twenty20 tournament and was actually doing a lot for the development of young talent by developing infrastructure in the respective islands. That of course was being fuelled by the funding you were pushing into the region through the different island boards. If you refer back to the press release at my announcement as a board member, that is very clear. Now that the funding has been totally cut off, because that is now the situation after the decision that was taken at the last board meeting January 4th 2008, I cannot justify still being a board member. Irrespective of the WICB having given you their assurance that money will still get to these boards through them, that will not be the case as I highlighted in the board meeting.

Sir Allen, these funds are all yours and I can understand the frustrations you must feel when you see that your good intentions have been taken advantage of by some of the organisations that your funds have gone to, but there are ways to deal with it without cutting it off completely. As I suggested at the board meeting, you have fourteen of us as Legends on your board with all the islands involved having a Legend and some, two Legends assigned to them. Why can't these Legends be responsible to some degree for the spending or disbursement of these funds? If I am a Legend on your board being remunerated as well as I am, with my obligations being just to attend one board meeting per month in addition to visiting an island or two for a few days each month, why can I not have the added responsibility of monitoring the funds coming from your organisation on whose board I sit? As a Legend, I don't require an auditor's qualifications to look at an invoice for a product, locate the product to make sure it has been purchased and authorise payment for that product. I am not dealing with a supermarket with hundreds of purchases and invoices. As for the argument that the Legends are not always available in the respective islands on a day-to-day basis, that is not a valid argument. Any invoice for a service provided will always have a payment period attached, whether 30, 60 or sometimes even 90 days for payment. Certainly a Legend can get to his island within that time period to get it sorted and authorise payment.

Anyway Sir Allen, the board has spoken and I am in the minority and by a huge margin. As I said at the beginning, my main reason for joining the board has been removed so I have to now remove myself.

I wish you and your organisation all the success you could ever hope for with the Twenty20 tournament and I will be happy to be in Antigua to support the tournament in person wholeheartedly and fulfil all of my obligations for this event. I believe, like you, that the Stanford Twenty20 tournament will be a huge success and thoroughly enjoyed by all who attend and watch on TV worldwide. And I hope that down the road it turns out as a financially successful programme while also continuing to grow in popularity. I know how much money you have thrown at it and as I have said on so many occasions, I hope it isn't in vain.

Sorry to be so long-winded, but I had to get it off my chest and let you know exactly how I feel. Although I am offering my resignation as of February 25th, if you would prefer it to be immediate, I am happy to comply.

Regards Michael Holding

Sir Allen tried to convince me to stay on the board with the line: 'Mikey, we are going to not just save the sport in the Caribbean, we are going to re-invent the sport in the Caribbean.' His plea fell on deaf ears, however, although I wasn't that deaf to not notice his reference to changing the sport in the Caribbean. Later his chants changed from making the West Indies the best in the world to making the West Indies the best Twenty20 team in the world. By stopping funding for the islands, we were not going to save cricket in the Caribbean – just because no-one could be bothered to put proper procedures in place to monitor the spending.

Sir Allen wanted me to stay on for the 2008 tournament, which I did, fulfilling my obligations to the best of my ability. I was present until the last ball was bowled in the final, won by

Trinidad & Tobago, at the Stanford Cricket Ground, and then I left. I didn't stay for the fireworks or the trophy presentation. I wanted to get away from it all as quickly as possible. I went straight to my hotel, checked out the next day and flew home, relieved that I would have nothing to do with Sir Allen again.

I suppose I should not have been surprised at the way it ended. Throughout my association with Sir Allen, there had been instances which suggested that if he was not getting his own way or his pride was dented in any way – which it was with the islands spending the money in the wrong way – he would overreact and we would see the other side of his character. An example arose just before the 2008 Stanford Twenty20 tournament when West Indies were delayed from returning from a tour of South Africa by a week, meaning that some players would miss the start of his competition.

When Sir Allen found out, he went ballistic. He had negotiated five clear weeks with the WICB for his tournament and thought he was being made a fool of. So what did he do? In a fit of pique, he called for the tournament to be cancelled. He got in touch with Laurie-Ann, whose company, don't forget, was organising the tournament, and told her to call a press conference in Barbados, at which he would explain why it was being called off.

Laurie-Ann emailed back later and gave details of the logistics of what would have to be done to cancel the tournament. By the end of this interaction, Sir Allen had cooled off and changed his mind.

If he could be reactionary, it was because of his temper. He would rant and rave, making people in his presence cower. As I said earlier, it could be quite frightening.

At the 2008 tournament, he lost it big time again, after a couple of young players (Devon Thomas/Kieran Powell) from the two professional teams that he had founded in Antigua and

Nevis were called up to play for West Indies Under-19s in the Youth World Cup in Kuala Lumpur. He didn't know the two had gone and when he found out he blew a fuse. He demanded to know why they were there playing for West Indies instead of his teams. He demanded they come back. They didn't, of course, but it just showed the regard in which he held our cricket. Their presence in an emerging West Indies side should have been something he was proud of because such recognition was what the professional sides were presumably set up for. But instead he decided to argue that he was being undermined and the WICB was being ungrateful. His argument was that he was paying these guys a wage and he would have to pay their medical bills if they got injured.

This was further evidence to me, although I had already written my resignation letter, that it was all about him, Allen Stanford, and 'his' cricket, not West Indies cricket. Unsurprisingly, not long after the decision to stop the funding, the pro teams that he set up were dissolved. Interestingly enough, this happened shortly after he signed the deal with the ECB for his 'Twenty20 for $20m'. He didn't need them anymore. The project was shelved. It was another bad blow for West Indies cricket and a damming indictment on Sir Allen's motives.

Throughout my dealings with Sir Allen, it became apparent that he was typical of many folk I have met with a lot of money. Thankfully, they are not all like that, but as I have travelled the globe, I have come across a few similar characters and they all hold the same attitude to life. They think they can buy anything. If they want something, they throw money at it and they get their way. If there is a problem, they throw money at it and it goes away. And all the while they want to be the centre of attention, making sure their ego is constantly boosted in line with their bank balances, going up by the minute with interest.

In October 2008, the 'Twenty20 for $20m Stanford Super

Series' took place with England meeting the Stanford Super-stars for the loot. Before the tournament began, I said it would be a farce and that I thought the ECB had become involved for all the wrong reasons. The ECB said it was getting involved, not because of the money it and hopefully their cricketers would be getting, but to help West Indies cricket. However, I was proved correct. Before the tournament had even ended, there were a few who understood what I was talking about.

Sir Allen was criticised for walking into the dressing rooms, having his own personal cameraman follow him around the ground and then there was the tomfoolery with the players' wives. The press back in the UK was riled by his behaviour, but goodness knows what would have been written had the full extent of Sir Allen's shenanigans been known.

The 'Twenty20 for $20m' only went ahead after an eleventh-hour agreement. There had been a dispute between the Stanford Group, the WICB and Digicel, which sponsored West Indies cricket and was unhappy that the Stanford Superstars were effectively a West Indies representative side, and that it was not getting the promotional rights to which it was entitled. Digicel took WICB to the London Court of International Arbitration because the Stanford match compromised its exclusive sponsorship rights. Of course, Digicel won its case against the WICB. Sir Allen was again furious because he had been denied the chance to sell sponsorship rights for the tournament to any company in direct competition with Digicel. I'm glad I wasn't around when he got that news.

Eventually Sir Allen and Digicel came to an agreement to allow the tournament to go ahead, with Digicel getting all that was due to it, while the WICB stayed quiet, having lost the case. The WICB did not have a representative at the match – won by the Stanford Superstars team, who humiliated England – which would have been odd had I not discovered

Sir Allen had 're-negotiated' his deal with the WICB. As I understand it, Sir Allen changed the terms of the original agreement. He insisted that the WICB give up its share of the $20 million, which was $3.5 million, the same as the ECB. He saw it as compensation for scuppering his sponsorship plans.

It was not just a one-off $3.5 million payment that WICB would not receive. It was for the same amount for each of the years 2008, 2009 and 2010 – the initial three years that the tournament was going to be held. So WICB will end up without a cent to its name, despite Sir Allen's proclamations that he was there to help West Indies cricket and that his tournament would revive cricket in the West Indies. I don't see how WICB being out of pocket by a total of $10.5 million by 2010 helped do that, do you? In fact, West Indies cricket would have been denied three times if you include the loss of money to the islands through his initial funding and the closure of the pro teams. But again I stress, it was 'his' money and so his to disburse – just don't try to pull wool over the public's eyes.

Of course, the WICB has said nothing publicly. I would assume that's because it's too embarrassed about the predicament it got itself into by ignoring Digicel's rights when dealing with Stanford. And although the ECB know about it, it has kept its mouth firmly shut, too, because the reason it used to justify hiring out its players to play in the tournament was, laughably, to benefit West Indies cricket. England's chairman Giles Clarke and chief executive David Collier will be reluctant to admit knowledge of a deal that will shame them, casting them as pawns in Sir Allen's game, but the agreement was with three parties, the Stanford organisation, the WICB and the ECB. All three knew the terms of the agreement. But let's not only cast the ECB in a bad light. It gave up US$500,000 out of its first $3.5 million to the WICB so that the WICB could pay Digicel's court costs for the case in London. This could have been at Stanford's insistence because it was included in the signed documents, but let's give the ECB the benefit of the doubt and say it did it by itself. How magnanimous.

For me this was the most distasteful part of the farce. I wouldn't mind if Sir Allen had been upfront with the public from the start; telling them he was in it to make money, boost his profile, further his companies and be at the centre of the glitz and glamour. Or maybe even just say nothing. That's fine. I wouldn't have had a problem with that; it was his project and his money (again, that's what we all thought at the time). But to dress it up as helping West Indies cricket was wrong.

At the end of the Twenty20 for $16.5m match, Sir Allen grabbed the microphone and shouted from a podium, 'We are back, we're going to take the world again! This programme is working!' It reminded me of the way a certain George W. Bush stood on an aircraft carrier claiming 'mission accomplished' during the Iraq war in 2003. Both men stood on a platform, both thought they were bringing unity, both claimed victory and both had ulterior motives. We know what happened in Iraq, and we saw what happened immediately after, when the West Indies lost 3–0 to Pakistan in the next ODI series. Both Bush and Stanford were rich men from Texas and further proof that no amount of money can buy class.

Later discoveries regarding Sir Allen and his financial empire brought to light by the Securities and Exchange Commission in the United States have caused a few comments from some interesting sources. All of a sudden, a certain cricketer involved in the 'Twenty20 for $20m' game in Antigua suddenly declared that he always thought Sir Allen was a 'sleazeball'. But apparently he didn't find him a big enough 'sleazeball' to prevent him from signing a lucrative contract with him to act as an ambassador for his tournament. Another cricketer, left out of the squad, who argued at the time that although out of that particular squad, he should still be a part of the sharing of the funds should his team win, all of a sudden found fault as well. He reportedly declared that he was glad it was all over, for he didn't like the way Sir Allen landed at Lord's with his helicopter and walked around as if he owned the place. Why didn't he express those thoughts before when he was arguing to share in the winnings? As I said previously, money can't buy class, but it can apparently buy lots of other things.

17

THE STATE OF WEST INDIES CRICKET

They say that form is temporary, but class is permanent. I am not too sure how that well-worn phrase would apply to the state of West Indies cricket today. Perhaps it would be that the only thing that has been permanent, or consistent, is a string of disappointing results, while the flashes of a brighter future have too often proved temporary.

Sure, it is a sad state of affairs. But if you are expecting me to bleat on while wringing my hands about the game I love in the islands I love, forget it. Not going to happen. I feel the pain and disappointment as much as anyone in the Caribbean when West Indies perform poorly, just as you do when the country or team you support does likewise in any sport. So I don't need to waste words going on about how it makes me feel because you know exactly what it is like.

Instead, I thought it would be better if I spent this chapter making some suggestions about what could be improved in the Caribbean to make the West Indies team better. Indeed, this chapter is the first of five which look at how our wonderful game has changed and what can be done to improve it. I'm well and truly on the soap box, folks.

I promise that I will try not to use another well-worn phrase, 'In my day we did it like this' too much, although do bear in mind that in my era – and a bit beyond – West Indies lost only one Test series between 1975 and 1995.

Perhaps that unprecedented success has contributed to the pain that so many now feel. Perhaps a generation or two got it in their heads that the only thing the West Indies cricket team did was win because they knew of nothing else. At the time of writing, West Indies have won two of their last 20 series. And I'm not including series victories over Bangladesh or Zimbabwe. They don't count – beating teams ranked below you is taken as a given.

I have not made that comparison to give my era a pat on the back or to try to make the current crop of players feel small or insignificant compared to past players. It is only to highlight that something, somewhere, has gone wrong.

What isn't one of the problems is the influence of American sports on Caribbean culture. This is becoming something of a cliché. I have lost count of the number of times I have heard observers suggest that Caribbean people are not interested in playing cricket because they favour basketball or baseball. For the record, Curtly Ambrose was spotted playing basketball and told, 'Hey, you'll make a good fast bowler.' He didn't hesitate when cricket was offered as an alternative and I use that example to illustrate that basketball has always been around; it's not a recent phenomenon.

The Americanisation of the islands is an easy target because an awful lot of American sports are shown on TV, but few locals sit down to watch them and then begin to dream of playing one of them professionally. It is just not a realistic goal for people of the region.

For me there are a few factors which have contributed to West Indies' slump. Of course the players have to take some responsibility. The WICB must take a greater share of the blame, though. Their administration and organisation have been amateur at best, but we'll come to those points later.

I want to start where West Indies cricket should start: the basics, the grassroots.

In my day (that pledge didn't last long), playing sport in general was on the brain as soon as you walked through the school gates. It was all we seemed to do, so much so that it is a struggle to remember if we ever did any studying. This is the difference. Today in Jamaica, and I'm using the island as my example because that's where I'm from and am familiar with, kids just do not play enough school cricket. It has not died out, but it is in a far from healthy condition. Some schools struggle to even find eleven children to make a team.

I attended Kingston College, which had four cricket teams. There was one for the Sunlight Cup, the senior team, and a second XI for that competition which played practice matches against the first XI and against other schools that had such a team. There was no recognised second XI competition; these games were just practice matches and a chance for those in this team to put pressure on the first XI members. Then there was the Colts competition for under-16s and below that the Junior Colts, which was for under-14s. If you were under 14 and good enough you played in both Colts teams, and if you were a Colts player and something special you played in the Sunlight Cup team. In my time there was one such gentleman who qualified for all. He has been mentioned on other pages – his name was Sydney Headley, another of the sons of the great George Headley. Sydney was young enough, but also brilliant enough to represent the school at all three levels at once.

The potential for development was huge. The more exposure you got to the higher standard, the more you improved. We would have inter-form competitions in our school as well. You know, 4b versus 4c and so on. Then there would be house cricket. I was put in Gibson House because my brother, Ralph Junior, was in it, and we would play against the other houses.

The whole point of the form and house games, apart from healthy exercise for youngsters, was for the sportsmaster to identify talent. It is easy to see how a structure like the one described was bound to throw up a few talented cricketers. The whole thing was taken very seriously, particularly the Sunlight Cup. Most of Jamaica's cricketers developed by playing in that competition and there was a great tradition between the high schools in Kingston: Kingston College, Wolmer's, who were our arch rivals, Calabar, St George's, Jamaica College and Excelsior to name a few, and then there was a separate competition for schools in the rural areas called the Headley Cup named after, you know who, yes the legendary George Headley. The winners of these two competitions then played each other to determine the champions of the island.

It is nothing like that now, though. I don't think high schools in Jamaica even have a Colts competition. And sportsmasters at schools are a dying, if not already dead, breed. The position of sportsmaster is one that a lot of schools can no longer afford in these harsh economic climes, and the days of volunteerism by teachers already on staff or 'old boys' returning to the school to give their time are fading fast.

This is our biggest problem. There are not enough opportunities for kids to play cricket. As a consequence, the school team doesn't necessarily represent the best cricketers in the school, but just merely the best of the few who choose to try out for the final XI. There could be, and I'm absolutely sure this is the case, a host of talented individuals who have been lost to other sports or just other endeavours through a lack of opportunity or for that matter inclination. Now multiply that by the number of high schools in the country and you realise how many are slipping through the net. But for all that, let's say you have a young guy who has shown some talent in his school team. How is he going to improve, learn about his strengths and weaknesses and test himself when the guys he is playing against are not as good as they should be? He's not. So his development is stunted and he gets to the next level without being properly tested and with faults that should have been corrected at an earlier stage of his development. This is a complaint even being echoed by various coaches at the West Indies Test team level. It is a simple theory: the more competition there is, the better the end product. It applies in sport just as it does in business.

I'll make it clearer still. If you are running a race and it becomes apparent that you are much faster than everyone else in that race, what do you do? You ease off, take the last few yards easy. So you don't improve because you are not being tested.

Every now and then a player comes along who proves such a theory wrong, but it is rare. Brian Lara is an example and he was a once-in-a-generation player. People who reckon that talent will always win out are totally wrong.

We need to get back to the 'the good ole days' (here we go again), when sports were compulsory in schools and there was an allocated paid sportsmaster. Governments of the region take note. There has been a lot of talk from Caribbean politicians that sport is an integral part of island and country development. Here is an opportunity for them to put their money where their mouths are: ALLOCATE SOME FUNDS IN THIS DIRECTION. West Indies cricket is important to the psyche and hence the development of West Indian people. Youth, sport (cricket), development. Sounds like a good target to me.

Of course, cricket faces other obstacles in the Caribbean these days. It is time-consuming, you need a large playing area to do it and as the economies in the islands change, focus also changes. Things are harsher financially now than they used to be.

There is not much that can be done to find room for people to play cricket. Over time playing fields have disappeared and when a government or council has the option to use space to create jobs by allowing a factory to be built, then they are going to give it the go-ahead instead of keeping it for sports. Private lands have also given way to housing developments, thus again decreasing space for the game.

Those fields behind Dunrobin Avenue where I learnt how to bowl fast are still there, but they have been greatly reduced in size. A school was built on the site some years back so there is less space to play. They then put a road through the remaining bit of land that used to house our community matches, which reduced the size of the somewhat inadequate boundaries as well. At least they seemed inadequate when certain hard-hitting batsmen were at the crease.

That's life, I guess. When I used to fly into Heathrow in my earlier years, before the playing fields started to disappear, I would see below all the green fields for football, rugby and cricket and wonder how many players the West Indies would produce if we had those facilities. I don't even bother to look these days.

The lack of space, coupled with the fact that the West Indies cricket team are struggling to inspire, does not help. People see the team performing poorly and they do not think, 'I want to play for West Indies.' It's the 'copy what you see' school of thought. Boys wanted to play for West Indies when they were doing well and there was huge interest in the game because of our success. Courtney Walsh was a product of that, and Ambrose I guess. If someone saw a similar specimen to those two today, they would be hesitant about going up and telling them to 'bowl fast' because cricket is not imprinted on the brain like it used to be.

With all that, it is obvious we have to be more proactive

when it comes to cricket in the Caribbean. Elsewhere in this book, I described how I played organised cricket for my community and club before I played for my school. That was because playing fields were available in these communities for such activities. That's no longer the case. As new communities are built, some on the aforementioned playing fields, the recreational facilities provided are basketball courts. Why? They are smaller, easier to maintain and hence are more cost-effective. Not, I repeat, because basketball is the new route to sports success in the Caribbean. With the playing areas disappearing, there is even more reason to get cricket back into the schools in a big way. These schools still have allocated playing fields and hence opportunities for organised competitions. From the schools, the identified talent can then move on to the clubs, which still have their playing fields. I guess in short what I am saying is that everything has to now come from an organised structure; we can't leave things to chance any longer and just hope that talented cricketers will fall out of the coconut trees.

The success of the Jamaican sprinter Usain Bolt in the Olympics was fantastic, and you can be certain that children seeing that want to grow up to be just like him. In the current climate, cricket struggles to capture the imagination in the same way.

So in short we have a recipe for failure. The growth of young talent is stunted, we have poor facilities and the West Indies team is not inspiring. It is a cycle that will only repeat itself. A vicious circle that won't break by itself.

Only two groups can put a stop to the wheel turning: the WICB and the players. If I'm going to apportion blame, and I am, I have no hesitation in putting most of it at the feet of the Board. It is responsible for cricket in the Caribbean and it is doing a very poor job, from top to bottom, from the president to the board members and the general employees. The Board has had horrendous problems employing the right kind of people. For example, it has never had a good stable secretariat; there is just too much turnover and since the days of the long-serving Steve Camacho ended, it has struggled to find a capable CEO. It's almost been like a revolving door: employing people, losing confidence in their ability to perform and then getting someone else in. And round and round we go. What a waste of scarce funds.

Most baffling of all is the attitude of the Board. It's almost a 'high and mighty' collective persona that it puts out there. Let me recount a story that highlights this exact point. Many complaints have come from companies and organisations connected to the sponsorship of West Indies cricket, and this is so damaging. One of the multinational companies that paid many thousands of dollars to be one of the sponsors of West Indies cricket had a promotion to do at the ground early one morning before start of play. The sponsor asked for some passes for the people involved to get into the ground for the event, the Board produced them, but spelt the name of the sponsor wrong. Incompetence. You cannot do that. I won't reveal the name of the company for fear of embarrassing them, but this gives you an idea of the unprofessionalism that we're talking about. Now why would any well-thinking company want to do business with an organisation as incapable as that.

But the WICB and its employees can't see what the problem is. You see, it behaves as if it thinks that because it has allowed a company the 'privilege' of getting involved in West Indies cricket, it doesn't need to be professional towards them or show respect. It thinks the company owes them, as if it is doing the company a favour. And that's a big problem.

In the modern era it is the other way around, and as soon as the Board comes to terms with the fact that amateur days are gone and ain't coming back, the better.

This leads us on nicely to what happened in Antigua in

February 2009 when West Indies hosted England for the second Test of a series on what can only be described as a beach. Due to the sandy outfield, only ten balls were possible before the match was abandoned, making West Indies cricket a laughing stock the world over.

Everyone with a modicum of understanding of the game saw it coming – and well before the scheduled first day. I walked on the surface and each time I put my foot down it would move a couple of inches. Before the toss, Jerome Taylor came up to me and asked, 'How do I run in to bowl on sand?' Can you believe it? What sort of problem is that for a young man to be facing on the morning of an important Test match? I could only suggest to him to try to be very light on his feet when running in, almost floating, because if he tried to battle against the sand he would tire and possibly injure himself. You shouldn't be telling a fast bowler such a thing because the art is all about running in with increasing pace and good rhythm to attain that power upon delivery.

At the time I felt ashamed. I still do. And that is the difference. After the Test was abandoned, I was quoted as saying that there would be no repercussions, no resignations and no sackings because no one takes responsibility. Guess what? At the time of writing seven months later, no one has paid the price. There is no culpability and no shame.

No doubt it will happen again in a few years. When a Test match, again involving England, was abandoned because of a dangerous pitch at Sabina Park in 1998, nobody was fired or replaced among the administrators. The Board just keeps stumbling along from one disaster to another.

The silence has been deafening since the Antigua 'beach' debacle. All that happened was the ICC banned cricket from being played on the ground for twelve months. A pointless gesture when none was scheduled to be played there anyway.

When there is no accountability off the field, how can there be any on it? If as a player you know you're playing for a bunch of clowns, it is harder to play at your peak. Yes, players should have pride in their own performance and want to do good for themselves and their profession, but that can soon fade away when you're surrounded by the incompetence of the people who employ you. Think of it in terms of your job. If you're going to work every day, slogging away for hours for people you regard as jokers, it is understandable if your work suffers. If you're lucky enough to work for people you respect, you'll go that little bit further and it won't be a chore.

I'd like to see the whole board restructured. Currently there are two representatives from each of the six regions. That is too many. You only need one from each region and then a vice-president and a president. That makes eight members. Four others should then be elected or co-opted onto the Board to have twelve members. These other four representatives should know the game, of course, but they should also be capable of bringing some professional expertise to the Board: specific business areas like marketing, finance or management. These people should be well respected in the region, want to be associated with success and want to disassociate from incompetence and failure. That should start things rolling. At the moment it's made up of people who don't bring enough to the table and basically are there just to be able to say they are board directors. Although to be honest, I fail to see why anyone should want to be identified as such during this calamitous period.

I can't leave this chapter without discussing the role of the players in our fall from grace. Often I get the feeling that the guys out on the field have either lost sight, or have never opened their eyes, of what it means to play for West Indies. These days I get the impression that it's just a job, a means to an end. Yes, it pays well and it's a good way to make a living, but it doesn't and shouldn't end there. Playing for the West Indies means a lot more. Again, I'm not blaming the cricketers of the modern generation if that's how they see it, but they need to be made aware of West Indies' history. This needs to be emphasised because it is not something that you become aware of as soon as you are selected. When I first got selected for the West Indies, my thoughts didn't suddenly flash to all the people in the Caribbean and around the world that I would be representing. There wasn't much thought about it on my first tour to Australia, either, but that soon changed.

On my first tour to England, I was still naïve about the people I was supposed to be representing. We were playing Surrey at The Oval in a three-day game, just a warm-up for the Test matches so there was supposedly no pressure on the team per se, but of course individuals were trying to impress for the Test matches later on. On the last day Surrey set us a target of 239 to win the match in about three hours. In our little gathering before resumption, Clive Lloyd told us that the plan was not to bother chasing, and when our openers, Alvin Kallicharran and Roy Fredericks, went out into the middle, they did so under strict instructions to get 'crease time'. Clive felt it was more important that batsmen got time in the middle and started to acclimatise to English conditions than winning the game. That squad of cricketers which toured in 1976 had several players who had played county cricket in England before, but some of us were green to it.

As usual, there were a large number of West Indians in the ground. As soon as it dawned on them that their side was not trying to win, they turned on us big time. They heckled and booed for three hours. No let up. Then they waited for us to come out of the dressing room at the end of the game so they could shout abuse as we got onto the bus, too. And that was quite a few hours after the game had ended because we hadn't rushed to leave the ground after play. In those days, there was the usual visiting of dressing rooms by opposition members, having a chat over a few drinks and general socialising, plus the cricket bags had to be packed again to move on to the next venue.

I asked Gordon Greenidge why the fans were being so hostile. He explained how they were desperate for us to win because being a West Indian in a different country could be hard, particularly in England at the time. Most felt like second-class citizens and they wanted to walk around with their heads held high because their countrymen had shown on the field of play what they were capable of. A winning West Indies team meant they didn't have to worry about getting the mickey taken out of them when they went to work.

A documentary is in production about West Indies cricket, which highlights the fact that the performance of the 1976 West Indies team in England was a highly influential factor in the demonstrations that took place all over England by West Indians looking for equality. They figured if their cricketers could beat England so convincingly, they could get more equality in society and on the streets. It made me understand how what we did brought some joy and purpose to people's lives and they wanted to be proud of us. That was a powerful motivation.

History has shown that times have obviously changed. West Indians don't have the same struggles in other countries as they did 40 years ago, but they still want and need to be identified with success. Cricket is the only thing we in the Caribbean do together. In every other endeavour, we participate as individual islands. Only in cricket can someone from an island that has never produced an international cricketer still identify with West Indies.

When all the youngsters come together for the regional tournament – under-19s or under-16s, or whatever – which is usually held on one island, they need to be sat down and told all about what it means to play for West Indies. It is not just a job, which is the way some players look upon it.

There are other advantages to getting players together at an early age. Often what people do not realise about the West Indies is that we are a disparate group of people. Islands are sovereign nations; they have their own flag, currency, government and policies. So the potential problems of throwing eleven guys from these different cultures and political backgrounds into a confined space are obvious. Cliques can form – as they have in the past – that have a detrimental effect on the team.

Get them sitting around together and they can understand that the fellow sitting opposite is just a human being. Remember how I met Andy Roberts when we were both on 12th man duty? We were vastly different, but in our formative years we were not stubborn or judgemental when it came to different cultures. We formed a bond, put our differences aside and became great friends. We didn't do too badly as an opening attack either.

If anything, all the different cultures in the Caribbean should be viewed as a strength because the West Indies unites like nothing else when the cricket team is doing well. Even islands who do not have a player represented are cheering on the team. When Usain Bolt won the 100 metres in the Olympics, the whole of the region celebrated and that was very special to see. But really it was a victory for Jamaica and the scenes we saw were nothing like what they would have been had West Indies produced something as special on a cricket field.

Players need to be made aware of all of these factors. Let's get back to teaching the Caribbean cricketing history in our schools and make people feel proud. Let's educate. We've come back to where we started, grass roots. It's that vicious cycle again.

You've probably noticed that I haven't mentioned anything about the West Indies Players Association, WIPA, which is currently in a war with the WICB and was the cause of a reserve team to face Bangladesh. To be honest, the less said about the organisation, the better. They claim to represent all the first-class cricketers in the Caribbean, but obviously don't. If they did, the WICB would not have been able to find so many willing souls to pick other teams when the strike was on, and until they organise themselves into a credible organisation, I won't be paying too much attention to them.

And another thing. WIPA keeps on chastising the Board, its members and employees in the public arena about its 'inappropriate' behaviour at various times, but never have I heard the WIPA even questioning its members when they act inappropriately. Just recently, it questioned the then incoming CEO Ernest Hilaire's comments regarding Chris Gayle's further role as captain of the West Indies because of his comments during the 2009 England tour. Chris Gayle stated that he wouldn't be too disappointed if Test cricket died and then backtracked when he realised the furore he had created.

Now this cannot be considered to be a responsible statement, yet I never heard of the WIPA writing to Chris Gayle to admonish him for such a damaging comment to come from the West Indies captain. It needs to take a look at itself, not just at the WICB. As I said before, when the WIPA gets its act together, I will consider them a credible organisation and therefore pay a bit more attention to them.

18

CHUCKING

Chucking. Throwing. Straightening of the arm. Whatever you want to call it, there is no doubt that the debate over suspect bowling actions has been one of the most divisive and controversial the game has known. I was once asked, 'Is throwing the most contentious issue in cricket today?' I supposed that it is, but in fact, it always has been. Have a leaf through the cricket history books and you'll read about a debate over whether a particular player had a suspect action in every decade since, well, 1872 I guess. I've spent some time trawling through some dusty old pages and found a list of players called for throwing in 'major matches' and the first was a guy called Tom Willis, who was playing for Victoria against New South Wales on 30 March that year. Since then, 21 bowlers have been 'no balled', the most famous of whom is Ian Meckiff, the Australian who was the first man to be called in a Test match in 1963, and, of course Muttiah Muralitharan, who had the dubious honour of being the second 32 years later.

It's a hot topic, to say the least, and it's been burning for a long, long time. I would hope that the fire is beginning to go out, however. Great progress has been made in making throwing a controversy only for the history books. This is as it should be, given the technology available. That the technology has been embraced has been down to the ICC, which has set up the Bowling Action Review Committee (BARC). Now I know what you are thinking, 'What's Mikey doing praising the ICC?', but don't worry, I've not taken leave of my senses. Where credit is due I'm more than happy to acknowledge it.

We are now (finally) in a situation where a bowler can be called or reported for throwing and within four weeks his action will be checked by biomechanics experts to see whether it conforms to the laws. He'll then either be given the green light to continue or, sadly, shown the 'stop' sign. This all sounds simple, but it has been a long process to get to such a stage. Six years in total, from 1999 to 2005. However, such an issue was never going to be simple and even now with all the work that has been done, there is still confusion and conjecture surrounding how we have got this far. So I wanted to take the time to bring clarity to a topic so often shrouded in smoke. This is what this chapter is all about.

I joined BARC after being recommended to the ICC by the West Indies Cricket Board. I was happy to do so. As a former fast bowler, I felt a good deal of pride and a sense of duty to help in whatever way I could. Having sat through many hours of meetings, videos of different bowlers' actions and lectures by sports scientists, I have a good understanding of the chucking row.

It wasn't always that way. When I joined I was clear on one thing. A chucker is a chucker and they have no place in the game. Several years later I still held that view. Well, let me tell you that I have learnt that it is not that straightforward.

When BARC was set up in 1999, it would be fair to say that our BARC was worse than our bite. We had no power. Sir Clyde Walcott was the chairman, Australia was represented by Bobbie Simpson, England by Doug Insole and umpire Nigel Plews, India by esteemed all-rounder Kapil Dev, New Zealand by John Reid, who played international cricket through the 1970s and 80s, Pakistan by Javed Burki, South Africa by Brian

Basson, Sri Lanka by Ranjan Madugalle, Zimbabwe by Andy Pycroft, and Steve Bucknor and Srinivas Venkataraghavan (or Venkat to most) for the umpires. David Richards, the ICC chief executive, the general manager Roger Hill and Clive Hitchcock, cricket operations manager, completed the committee.

Back then a bowler would be reported to us, we would look at his action on video (this will sound a bit backward given the advances but I'll explain later) and then we'd decide whether the arm had straightened or not. Our only power if we found this guy guilty was to say to his Board, 'You should stop playing him and do work on his action.' This was a recommendation, no more.

Sometimes the Board paid no attention whatsoever. The player continued to be picked, illegal action or not. The Boards were not particularly keen, either on setting up the rec-ommended bowling advisory panels to monitor their own crick-eters or stopping suspect bowling actions at their source, domestic cricket. Some took it on, others didn't, including my own board in the Caribbean, the West Indies Cricket Board.

A lot of people misunderstood what the committee was there for. Sometimes you had situations when a player's action was reported and reviewed by the committee and we said, 'Yes, he's fine.' But this didn't mean he was fine forever and ever, amen. We had concerns that guys who might have done the rehab would suddenly think they were untouchable and were clear for life. Not the case. It was a 'take each ball as it comes' situation.

Eventually after BARC told the ICC chief executive com-mittee that we were achieving little, things did change. Any player found to have an illegal action had to be withdrawn immediately and we were also instructed to sit down to go through the entire procedure, from a player being called or reported to analysis of the action, a ban and remedial work.

Benson and Hedges Cup, 1985, Essex v Derbyshire at Chelmsford (quarter final). I am being congratulated by my Derbyshire team-mates after bowling Graham Gooch for 0. (Patrick Eagar)

Courtney Walsh, 1988. England v West Indies (Colorsport)

Daren Powell and Jerome Taylor of the West Indies chatting to me during the West Indies' nets session at Headingley on 24 May 2007. (Tom Shaw/Getty Images)

A groundsman digs up the run-ups after play is abandoned during the Second Test at the Sir Vivian Richards Cricket Ground, Antigua, 13 February 2009. (Gareth Copley/PA Wire/PA Photos)

Shoaib Akhtar, Cricket World Cup 1999 (Patrick Eagar)

Muttiah Muralitharan, Cornhill Test, England v Sri Lanka at The Oval, 1998. (Patrick Eagar)

Umpires Darrell Hair (second left) and Billy Doctrove inspect the ball with Inzamam-ul-Haq of Pakistan during day four of the Fourth npower Test match between England and Pakistan at The Oval on 20 August 2006. (Shaun Botterill/Getty Images)

Australia's Adam Gilchrist, right, walks off the field after he was given out lbw while the Sri Lankan players celebrate during the Tri Nations cricket one-day match between Australia and Sri Lanka in Melbourne, Australia, 13 January 2006. (AP Photo/Tony Feder)

Shane Warne and members of the Rajasthan Royals cricket team wave to crowds during a street parade in Cape Town by teams competing in the Indian Premier League Twenty20 cricket tournament, 16 April 2009. (Reuters/Mike Hutchings (S Africa Sport Cricket/Action Images)

And I thought fast bowling was tough! I learnt an awful lot when running my gas station and am forever grateful to the people of Kingston for their support.

From left: Ian Chappell, Ravi Shastri, Tony Greig, Richie Benaud, me, Mark Mascarenhas and Sunil Gavaskar at the 1996 World Cup.

My work is
never done.
Preparing for a
post-match
presentation in
Zimbabwe.

Enjoying winding down on my first comms job in
Australia. John Gayleard is at the back, Tony Grieg on
the extreme right, Reds Perreira is second right.

Mark Mascarenhas was a good man and he is
missed. Here I am with his two sons.

Chris Gayle of the Superstars and Sir Allen Stanford pose with the cheque during the Stanford Twenty20 Super Series 20/20 on 1 November 2008 in St Johns, Antigua. (Tom Shaw/Getty Images)

(*below left*) Richie Benaud (Graham Morris/Cricketpix Ltd)

(*below right*) Tony Cozier (Graham Morris/Cricketpix Ltd)

Sky commentators (back l to r): Michael Holding, David Gower (front l to r): Nasser Hussain, David Lloyd, Michael Atherton and Ian Botham celebrate Sky's 100th Live Test Match during day one of the Fourth npower Test match between England and Pakistan at The Oval on 17 August 2006. (Tom Shaw/Getty Images)

Working with Ian Chappell, Barry Richards, Sanjay Manjrekar on one of Mark Mascarenhas' productions in Los Angeles. Australia 'A' v India 'A'.

Most mornings during the English summer I can be found on Newmarket Gallops. Here I am sharing a laugh with Henry Cecil, Michael Bell and Sir Michael Stoute. (Trevor Jones)

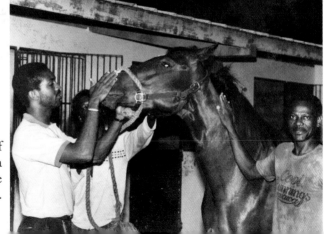

The power and beauty of horses captivated me from a young age and it was a pleasure to try my hand at ownership.

Not the most elegant of jocks! I put Kribensis, who won the Champion Hurdle, through his paces at Sir Michael Stoute's yard.

I hated touring India on my first visit but now I can't get enough of the place. Laurie-Ann and I look the typical tourists in front of the Taj Mahal.

Become a cricket commentator and see the world! Laurie-Ann and me in Sri Lanka and look-out point at the Cape.

Simple? Well, easy now, let's not get carried away . . .

Under the new powers, the first player to be banned was Shabbir Ahmed from Pakistan. He was reported immediately following his one-day international debut when he picked up three wickets against West Indies in a one-day tournament in Toronto in September 1999. It was not highly publicised because, not surprisingly, few people knew about Shabbir. Things got sticky, however, when in December 1999 a ban was also handed out to Pakistan's Shoaib Akhtar. Big-name player. And of course it was huge news that he had been banned for chucking.

A month later the Pakistan Cricket Board appealed against the decision. The next thing I was aware of was that Jagmohan Dalmiya, the ICC president at the time who hailed from India, was in the news stating that the ban on Shoaib had been reversed. As far as I am aware, there was no consultation with the cricket committee, so I presume that it was the action of the executive board of the ICC. Now why was that done, I wonder? Anything to do with politics or was it just the pressure brought because of the high-profile individual?

In February 2000 the executive board reversed its decision to ban players. We were back to square one, although this was perfectly understandable because it was clear that when telling a cricketer he couldn't play, we were denying him the opportunity to earn. Lawyers would get involved as soon as you started to ban players and deprive them of their livelihood without an acceptable transparent process.

So four months after the executive committee granted the bowling action panel power to ban players, we were overhauling the entire process. The next step was for the ICC to set up a further review and a sub-committee, which included myself, Malcolm Speed, the ICC CEO, Imran Khan, Peter Willey, Sunil Gavaskar and Nishantha Ranatunga. What was agreed –

via video conference in October 2000 – was a revised three-stage process to deal with suspect bowling actions. The aim was that it should act decisively after a player had been reported and that it was fair. All world cricket boards would have to employ bowling advisors and the ICC would agree to set up a panel (a new one called the Bowling Review Group) to deal with the third and final stage.

Stage One consisted of the umpires producing a report of a suspected bowler – having sought out footage from the host broadcaster, which would be couriered to the ICC within 24 hours – and the match referee confirming the player would be subject to a review of his action. The home board's bowling advisors would read the report and work with the bowler to fix the problem. Within six weeks they produce a report, which is sent to the ICC. Throughout this period the bowler was still allowed to continue to play.

Now on to Stage Two. If the player was reported (and by the way I should point out that at no time during these stages was power taken away from the umpires. If they wanted to 'no ball' someone who obviously had an illegal action in a match, they could do so) again within twelve months of the first report, the ICC would talk with the home board and send its own advisors to work on his action. A further detailed assessment would be filed by an ICC advisor within three months. Again, the bowler was still allowed to play because of this fear of being sued. So you can see where the flaws were. If he was still playing and a chucker, he was gaining an advantage. If he was a fast bowler, he could do physical harm with a chuck.

Stage Three was only reached – and it would take 18 months for a player to get so far – if a third report was filed. Then the Bowling Review Group would meet with the player to discuss the previous two reports, video footage and any further evidence supplied by the player and his board. Once that was out of the way, a vote was taken on whether the player's action was illegal. If the majority said it was, he was banned for twelve months.

These stages were sensitive. They were not draconian. They were there to help bowlers. They didn't throw players onto the professional scrapheap. However, they didn't really work. So 21 months later, they were scrapped.

By September 2002 we had just two stages. Stage One remained pretty much the same but Stage Two was different. Once reported, the bowler would have to submit to independent ICC analysis conducted by a biomechanics expert. We were now seeing science lending a huge hand. This expert had to be from a country other than the bowler concerned and he had to work fast. He had four weeks from the initial report to complete his analysis. If the bowler was found to be straightening the arm, then it was an immediate ban, only to be lifted once he had proved that he had fixed the problem.

The only time now that the bowler is seen by the Bowling Review Group – and it hasn't happened yet – is if he doesn't accept the findings. That ain't gonna happen. Good luck arguing against science.

The process worked. But don't breathe a sigh of relief just yet, guys, because I have a bit more 'legislation' to explain, a rule which has had people scratching their heads, suggesting foul play and providing more and more fuel for what remained the most blistering of topics. It was a new law which had to define throwing.

In the summer of 2004 during the Champions Trophy in England, the ICC commissioned the biomechanics people to study the degree to which every single bowler in the tournament straightened his arm (the bowling arm cannot straighten by more than 15 degrees). At the time, it would have been perfectly reasonable to predict that the high-powered camera lenses and super slo-mo would reveal only a handful, if that many, of 'guilty' bowlers. The result couldn't have been further from this.

A committee was set up to hear the findings and we were summoned to Dubai to listen to the biomechanics experts speak, watch video footage and pore over all manner of statistics. Going into that meeting, I remained staunch in my belief that if you chucked, you should be chucked out of the game. Straightening is straightening, I told myself, and I didn't care by how much. Well, get this, only two bowlers were shown NOT to be straightening their arm. One was Ramnaresh Sarwan – good friend or not, I'm struggling to suppress a laugh by calling him a bowler – and the name of the other escapes me. Even the great Glenn McGrath, who took 949 international wickets, was shown to be straightening his arm by 12 degrees. I would argue that no one sitting in the stands would have ever thought that of him. A revelation. McGrath, and many others, was a 'chucker' according to the historic laws of the game. In this instance, they had been proved to be archaic.

We were all stunned. Poor old Angus Fraser, the former England bowler, a member of the group summoned to Dubai, nearly fell off his chair and the bowlers in the room were all left wondering, 'How much did my arm straighten then?' More importantly, having been so sure previously that chucking was chucking, I was now convinced, just as everyone was, a measurement was needed to bring the laws up to date.

What we had to address, therefore, was the acceptable level of straightening. I say 'we', but in fact the decision to go with 15 degrees was based purely on what the boffins told us, people like Marc Portus from the Australia Institute of Sport, Cricket Australia, Professor Bruce Elliott from the University of Western Australia and Dr Paul Hurrion from Quintic Consultancy Ltd. These guys did the measurements in that 2004 tournament and lectured to us all in Dubai about the problems involved.

True to form for the historic chucking row, people decided that 15 degrees had been set because it had been reported that Muttiah Muralitharan, the highest Test wicket-taker, straightened by 14 degrees. The conspiracy theorists couldn't believe their luck. 'How convenient that the ICC had decided on 15 degrees when the greatest wicket-taker ever straightened by 14', they said. 'Best make sure cricket's finest bowler is unaffected', they said. It is perhaps a plausible theory given the way the ICC has sometimes operated. However, it is not true. Having sat in that room and seen and heard all the evidence, I can tell you for sure that it had nothing to do with Muralitharan. It was completely down to what the experts told us. They said that the human eye, normal 20/20 vision, cannot see any straightening less than 15 degrees. Television cameras can pick it up with their slo-mo, but the guy in the stand, the fielder at mid-off and the umpire at square leg would not spot anything untoward.

To make things uniform and fair, we couldn't start banning players for less than 15 degrees when in the past, way back to our friend Tom Willis in 1872, the umpires had nothing to go on but their eyes. History dictated that it was the human eye that set the limit, not the technological one. To do anything else would have meant rewriting those history books.

As I said earlier, Glenn McGrath straightened by 12 degrees and with the naked eye, he was perfect. You can't start calling bowlers like him chuckers. Others were straightening to only a small degree, but it was still straightening, so we could no longer use that as carte blanche.

I'll break it down a bit further – here comes the science bit. The biomechanics say it was noticed that elbow extension of less than 10–12 degrees was not discernible to the naked eye, even when viewed at the slowest of speeds. At around 12–15, a certain amount may be noticeable, but still only when viewed in slow motion. When it rises above 15, it becomes easier to spot.

They tested our eyes by splitting up bowlers into groups. We watched bowlers who had a straightening of 12 degrees or less, then 12–15 degrees and finally those who were 15 or more. We weren't told beforehand who fell into which group and there were a few shocked faces again when the details were revealed.

What was not taken in account was this issue of hyper-extension, when a bowler's arm bends back the other way from elbow to wrist. This was not measured with regard to the 15 degrees. Shoaib Akhtar, among others, hyper-extended, although that did not make our decision to ban him that first time at all wrong, in my opinion.

With all this in mind, just think how blatant a chuck had to be to be called in the old days. When I was playing I can't remember anyone being called, but there were always rumours about people and you'd think, 'Hey, that guy doesn't look quite right.' The old naked eye again.

So having read all this detail, I'm sure you will agree that we have made progress. Sure, a lot of the time it was frustrating when we appeared to be taking one step forward and two back, but we consoled ourselves that it had to be right for the sake of players' careers.

Today, I think we're as good as we can be, or as much as the technology will allow. There is no longer a Bowling Action Review Committee or a Bowling Review Group and that has to be for the best. Now it goes directly to the biomechanics guys. It's not opinion, it's measurement.

Of course, you can't please everyone. There are some who say that because players are having their actions tested in laboratories, the measurements cannot be accurate given it's not a match situation. Well, they are right it isn't a match situation, but what do they want? Bowlers running in to the crease in a

Test match in just their shorts, with movement sensors stuck all over their body and cameras filming from about ten yards away? It's not feasible. So the ICC has done its best to replicate what it's like in the middle. Anyone who bowls at 90 mph in a match has to bowl at 90 mph in the lab. If you're a spin bowler, they make sure that you're putting the maximum revolutions on the ball. If the bowler doesn't match his pace in the middle or his effort in imparting spin when in the lab, he is not cleared for return to the game. It is finite stuff and highly accurate. The only shadowy aspect of it all is that the ICC has seen fit to decide to ban certain deliveries from bowlers if they think that particular delivery is illegally delivered. When this is the case though, the umpires and entire cricketing world are made aware of the situation and all eyes are then on that bowler and his deliveries. I am sure you can see there are a few problems associated with such a stance, but thankfully so far so good.

When BARC was set up in 1999, we had nothing as advanced to base our recommendations on. We were looking at bowling actions from different angles (from the front, behind the arm and another from square leg) on videotape. The tapes were sent to all members of the committee, we'd watch them in our different corners of the globe and then we'd link up via conference call to get each other's opinion. It wasn't ideal. People would talk over one another and the point would be lost. Sometimes no one would speak, thinking another was just about to open his mouth. It was rare that there were disagreements, though.

This might raise a few eyebrows, but one guy who definitely didn't cause contention among the committee was Muttiah Muralitharan. He had been called seven times in three overs by Darrell Hair in a Test match in Melbourne as early as 1995, and there had long been whispers about his action. He was eventually reported to us, along with his bowling teammate,

Dharmasena, after a 1999 one-day tournament in Sharjah. We were unanimous about both men. Dharmasena was chucking and Murali was not.

Murali's arm looked awkward because of the deformity in his arm. It looked bent and everyone was under the impression it was straightening. However, when you examined it, it started bent and finished bent. It didn't start bent and straighten. And if it was straightening, it was minimal and only visible with slo-mo and your eyes straining. There was hardly anything to worry about.

There is something to worry about with his doosra, however. In my opinion the real problems with regard to his action, and the controversy deepened, only when he developed the doosra. Whatever minimal straightening there was before the doosra was enhanced with the doosra. It was greater. It has been easier to spot with the naked eye. It was no longer an illusion.

If you look at the other bowlers who have tried to bowl the doosra – Harbhajan Singh for one and most recently, Johan Botha of South Africa – they all have been reported and told the action is not right, that the arm was straightening too much. Botha has been banned from bowling doosras and can play on. I've got no problem with that because he would be mad to try to slip one in during a game and risk a ban. So what if bowlers are in their 20th over of the day in a Test and they reckon they can get away with one? The umpire, who will know all about the player's history, can call him or make a note on his jotter pad to check the replays.

But when it comes to Murali, are we meant to believe that he is the only man who can legally bowl it? It reminds me of a hypothetical story Mum used to tell us kids to make a point. She would say: 'This very proud mum was at a scout parade watching her children march around the parade ring. Her son was out of step and when a friend brought it to her attention, her response was that "No, he is fine – it's the other scouts who are all out of step.". Sure, please give me a break.

Still, it is not my intention to relight the fires under this controversy. The flames, if anything, have been doused and if the doosra is to be the one spark that threatens to ignite every now and then, we will have to live with it.

19

ICC MAN

It would be fair to say that my relationship with the International Cricket Council has been an odd one. I revelled in the work for the bowling actions committee, getting a tremendous sense that I was giving something back to the game, but all the while I remained a fierce critic of the organisation that I was 'working' for.

In my role as a television pundit I do not deliberately set out to make sure that my backside is off the fence. As mentioned earlier in this book, if I see something not quite right then I have my say, regardless of any loyalties people might think I have or should have. Even though I was involved with the inner workings of the game's governing body, it never stopped me shouting when they got something wrong.

Often in a day's commentary, as well as just describing what is happening on the field, we will talk about all manner of things affecting the game off it, especially during quiet moments. And the ICC's actions over the past few years have filled many a minute.

I have been one of their most vocal critics. It was the case before I joined the bowling actions committee, during and after. So forthright was I that I never thought I would be asked to sit on a committee again after the bowling actions committee had been disbanded. So when I got a call in 2007 from Brian Murgatroyd, the ICC's media man at the time, asking me to join the new cricket committee, I thought a good friend of mine was having a little joke at my expense. You see, I have known Murgers for many years in his different roles, at Sky in the commentary box supplying us commentators with excellent statistics, through to media manager for both the English and Australian cricket teams, to the ICC.

'Very funny, Murgers,' I said. 'You've had your fun, now run along.' But he was for real. I reminded him that I had been far from easy on the ICC before and I was sure he had to be joking. But he told me it was the real thing, no joke.

'No Mikey, it's come straight from the chief exec.'

'In that case, Murgers,' I replied, 'you know me, always willing to serve.'

Sadly, things did not work out and rather than spending some time helping to move the game on in a positive fashion, I eventually found the experience a negative one that gave me more bullets to fire at the ICC. But of course it was not all bad.

I resigned from that committee because of the ICC's complete lack of respect for the laws of the sport we were all supposed to love when they overturned the result of the infamous forfeited Test match at The Oval in 2006 between England and Pakistan. They did it for political gain, without a thought to the damage they were doing to the game itself. It was all about people doing favours for each other. It was about as cheap a shot as you could get.

It made a mockery of the committee, which had been set up to truly represent every aspect and shareholder of the game. The committee was therefore a good idea. I had been asked to represent television. Simon Taufel was there to represent umpires; Mickey Arthur the coaches; Mark 'Tubby' Taylor sat for former players; Keith Bradshaw was there from the MCC; Dilip Mendis, the Sri Lanka chief executive, represented the CEOs of the full members; Tim May, the Federation of

International Cricketers' Associations; Steve Tikolo from Kenya represented the associate members; David Kendix the statisticians; Sunil Gavaskar, who needs no introduction, was chairman, and David Richardson, the ICC general manager of cricket, also sat on the committee.

From this list of names you can see that it was a thoughtfully selected committee representing all the different stakeholders in the game. There were some strong characters there and men who had been very successful in their careers on the field and then also off it.

In May 2007 I attended the first meeting in Dubai and was really excited to be involved in something where I thought I could make a difference and there was a second meeting in May 2008. I was not around for the third, having quit after the England-Pakistan debacle. Short and not so sweet, I guess. But as I said before, it wasn't all a bad experience. The first two meetings were very fruitful, what with the gentlemen previously named involved, and lots of good ideas that would benefit the game resulted from those deliberations.

For those who need their memories refreshing, the England-Pakistan debacle I referred to was about England being awarded the Test at The Oval because Pakistan had refused to take to the field after tea after the umpires Darrell Hair and Billy Doctrove, rather a forgotten man in the scheme of things, had accused Pakistan of tampering with the ball. I was commentating on the Test match for Sky, and during the controversy and chaos, I made it public knowledge that I was in support of Inzamam-ul-Haq, the Pakistan captain, for his action because I thought they were very serious accusations. What Hair and Doctrove had accused Pakistan of was cheating. It wasn't a warning or a suspicion. When five runs were added to England's total, the umpires had effectively charged Pakistan and found them guilty. Crystal clear. It was a harsh decision.

To make such a decision, you need some strong proof and I was of the opinion that Inzamam didn't think his team had committed the crime they were accused of, and of course it was later ascertained that the umpires didn't have enough evidence to judge Pakistan guilty. I was in support of Inzy demonstrating that he was totally against what had taken place and that his team had been badly treated, just like Clive Lloyd all those years ago in New Zealand. Some may say he could have made his displeasure known some other way instead of refusing to carry on, but I would not question his method of protest because being accused of cheating cannot be taken lightly. At the same time I knew that Inzamam must have known that there would be repercussions about keeping his men in the dressing room. People in the past, present and future believe there are some unjust laws and as such they may demonstrate against them. Sometimes change is brought about through these actions, but you know when you take such action there will be consequences (Lloyd did remember) and you must be prepared to accept them. Inzamam probably didn't know what they would be, but he knew they would come.

When the consequences, repercussions or whatever came from the ICC, Pakistan would have to accept them, whether they be forfeiting the game, a ban for Inzamam or a raft of fines. If the punishment was draconian, they could appeal. The punishment should fit the crime, whether on or off the field of play.

As we know, the action was that Pakistan had forfeited and the match was awarded to England. That was exactly what the laws of the game stipulated. The correct decision. Not draconian. Case closed thank you very much.

Well, not quite. During the second cricket committee meeting in May 2008, a proposal was put forward by Keith Bradshaw, who represented the MCC, that The Oval Test result of an England win should be revisited with the view of possibly changing it to a draw. But although it came from Bradshaw, the feeling in the meeting was that it wasn't really coming from the MCC. It seemed he was just the conveyor of the sentiment. I wonder who asked for it to be brought to the meeting? And of course the MCC itself came out very strongly against the decision to change the result after it was announced.

The proposal was thrown out unanimously within seconds. I've had longer conversations with people asking me for the time. None of the committee guys even gave it a second thought. As far as we were concerned, the laws were there and they had been used. Next item on the agenda please.

As I've said before, committees only recommend to the executive committee of the ICC. But none of us who sat around that table would have believed that our unanimous proposal that the motion to overturn the result should be thrown out would be completely ignored. But that is exactly what happened. The executive ignored its own committee, its own director of cricket, David Richardson, who sat on it, and ripped apart the stitches of the game's comfort rug: the laws. Well, that was it for me. A load of suits who didn't play the game just arbitrarily going against the laws? Time for me to go.

I believe it was all done for political expediency, a matter of people doing favours so other things would be done in return. I can't go into more detail about that, but it was the background. I believe that historically this has been a huge problem with the ICC, of course; just cast your mind back to the situation when Shoaib Akhtar was banned for throwing. I believed that to be the case then and still do today.

The ICC's disregarding of the laws was not something I wanted to be involved with. I also felt that, although inadvertently, I had been cast in a bad light through collective responsibility. Not in my name, as they say. I was completely dumbfounded when I found out. In fact I was fuming as I knew what I had to do, but at the same time I regretted that I had to do it. I had enjoyed being involved with the committee and being in the company of the illustrious gentlemen who sat with me. My resignation first became public knowledge when I announced it on Sky Sports during a domestic match in England. It had not been the plan, but during a break in play, I was in the studio with Charles Colville and he asked me what I thought of the decision. By then I had already written and emailed off my resignation so I saw no reason to evade the question. He looked a little taken aback when I said: 'I have just written my letter of resignation to the ICC cricket committee because I cannot agree with what they've done. That game should never, ever be a draw.'

Eventually the decision was reversed, following a proposal by the MCC and because there was such a backlash. I am glad that common sense and what is right won out in the end. People approached me after that to ask whether I'd go back to the committee. Of course everyone knows I haven't and I won't. If people can do things like that willy nilly, then they are liable to do it again. And that means I would have to resign and I can't keep resigning from things, it wouldn't make sense. I am not in the business of making myself look foolish.

I was also disappointed that more people on the committee didn't make their opinions known publicly. Some had spoken to me about it in private and I knew they were against the actions of the ICC executive, but they kept quiet. They never joined me in publicly condemning the action. Remember, we unanimously refused to consider changing the result at our meeting. This was very puzzling to me. None of those guys on that committee were shrinking violets. If they had something to say, they would say it. I remember so many good, strong personalities in those meetings, being quite firm on many issues.

I am still perplexed about it. I guess they thought I had said and done enough and thought they needn't join in, but I had hoped for some vocal support from some other committee members.

But an even greater disappointment, as I write now, is that I have received no acknowledgement from the ICC of my letter of resignation. No word from the ICC to say, 'Oh good riddance, we're glad you're gone' or maybe, 'Thanks for your service.' But we see in the press that I've been replaced by someone else. Hell, it doesn't trouble me personally, but it troubles me when an organisation responsible for a great game behaves like this. Billions of dollars pass through the ICC coffers and if they are not acknowledging such letters even for their own simple housekeeping, you wonder what else they should be doing but aren't, and cricket will eventually come off the worse.

I have since seen David Richardson and Haroon Lorgat, the chief executive of the ICC, at matches and both have discussed the issue with me off the record and tried to explain to me why certain things went on, but there has been no official word from the organisation about my resignation. I would like to believe that it just slipped through the net and it's not the way they operate but even so, it would not have if they were as organised as they should be.

It's the politics, unfortunately, which are to blame. The ICC is rooted in them. As you may know, it was called the Imperial Cricket Conference at one point, dominated by England and Australia, who had veto votes. Then they decided to make it more of a democratic process by renaming it the International Cricket Conference and each country then had one vote. That hasn't really worked though because you have people trying to manipulate voting and the politics really taking hold. Some countries always support certain other countries and form voting blocks. Zimbabwe lost their Test status, but not their full membership, and hence keep their voting power. I wonder why?

What can be done? Perhaps we should take a look at how FIFA, football's governing body, which is a more powerful and useful organisation than the ICC, is run. FIFA has the power to dictate to the footballing nations around the world for the betterment of the game. The ICC can barely tell the tea lady what to do.

What I like about FIFA is the sense of democracy. Brazil have won more football World Cups than any other country, but as an individual nation do they have more power than, say, Australia, who have won zip? No. That's how it should be. Just because one country has won more tournaments, has the most famous players or the strongest economy shouldn't mean that they get more of a say. That's the level ICC needs to get to.

Until something changes, the ICC will only get weaker. As an entity it is threatened by insignificance. Cricket needs a ruling body that is strong, functional and proactive, not a react-ive one manipulated by some.

Goodness knows I'm not the man to help make that happen. It saddens me to say that because I loved working on the bowling actions committee. We did a lot of good work and most of the recommendations put through were accepted. The subsequent cricket committee was a great innovation too and it will continue to do a lot of good work, for there are people on it who are prepared to think deeply about the game, are not afraid to go down radical paths or to put meaningful changes in place.

Almost every change you now see in the game, whether playing conditions or laws, has been instigated by the cricket committee. By people sitting down, analysing and really working hard. The umpire review system is probably the best case in point. The amount of time and effort spent examining the positives, negatives, potential boons and pitfalls, was tremendous. It was extensive and nothing was left to chance. When this system gets into full swing it will work well. The more it is used and the better people understand it, it'll work. I have one reservation though: I am hearing through the grapevine that the ICC intends to increase the number of referrals allowed by each team. I believe if they have too many, it could encourage frivolous referrals where teams know they can waste a few hoping for the best, instead of it being used for what it was created for. That is, to get rid of the really bad mistakes, 'the howlers'. At the moment, teams seem to be using it incorrectly, trying to change decisions that have gone against them and are borderline. If the umpires apply the principles correctly, that is, only ask the onfield umpire to change his decision if there is irrefutable evidence from the technology showing that it was wrong – NOT IF HE THOUGHT IT MIGHT BE WRONG OR COULD BE WRONG – then teams will soon understand how to use it properly. It takes understanding from both parties, the players and the umpires.

Another positive I can see coming out of this new system is the prospect of home umpires being allowed to officiate again in Test matches, instead of how it stands at the moment, only ODIs. The independent umpires panel came into force because of the perceived idea that home umpires were making 'home-town' decisions. With the referral system, it won't matter if the standing umpires are from any of the countries involved because to counter the perceived bias, the third umpire who would be adjudicating on the referrals would be independent of both teams. His final decision could not be seen as being biased towards 'his' team. This situation, I am sure, would make more umpires more inclined to want to be a part of the elite panel as it would guarantee less time away from home and family. This is something many complain about, and with more umpires to choose from, the better the standard of umpiring in the long run as the cream rises to the top.

What about the changes in the one-day game, where you have the powerplays and the batting team picking when they can take a powerplay? That is from the cricket committee as well. It was a great rule change to make the one-day form of the game more exciting and to get the captain and batsmen thinking instead of one or the other dominating.

The England v Pakistan issue aside, the committee has worked well because it is the most democratic process the ICC has ever had in place. The different people from the different shareholdings are not trying to force things through so they can feather their own nests or make things exclusively better for the area they represent. They understand that they are there to listen to all cricketing walks of life and come up with the solutions for the good of the game and everyone.

The umpires were against the review system coming in, but they were able to hear the voices from all these different spheres. Before they would have seen only their point of view and dug their heels in.

Do you know what? Having put those thoughts down in writing, I'm beginning to miss being part of it. I'd love to still be doing it. But always, lurking in the shadows, will be the politicians just biding their time before emerging to have their fateful say. As I said, I want to serve this game, but not under those conditions.

20

CHANGES

Change is not a word many people like. It makes them feel a little uneasy. 'What was wrong with the way things were?' they might say. As an old fogey (I don't mind admitting to that, folks), I will occasionally lend my voice to the chorus. I'm not quite in the realm of demanding my pipe and slippers at an appointed time each day or getting in a huff if something isn't done the way I'm used to, but as far as cricket is concerned, I often pine for days of old, or specifically how cricket used to be played.

My dislike of the potential impact of the Twenty20 format on cricket is well documented. Arguably it is the greatest change we have seen to the sport since the Kerry Packer revolution. I'm sure it will continue to have a huge impact as the years roll on.

There have been more subtle changes, though. Rules, regulations, the way the game is broadcast, training regimes, the fitness of players and their attitudes are all different from my era. They will be different in 20 years too. Some of the changes I am quite happy with, as I've said, others less so – the good, the bad and the ugly if you like. That's life, though, and I believe they say that if you are through with change, you are through with life.

One of the greatest changes for good has been the improvement in umpiring, thanks to the ICC setting up the Elite Panel in 2002. Initially there were eight umpires chosen and that number has now grown to 12. A commitment from the ICC to pick the cream of the crop for Test and one-day international matches should be applauded. More important, however, has been the rule that home umpires were not allowed to umpire in Test matches and only one was allowed in one-day internationals. Oh for such a ruling in Sydney in 1976 or Dunedin in 1980! True, mistakes are still made and will continue to be made (after all they are still human), but the perception of bias disappears with neither standing umpire associated or connected to the competing teams. As we all know, perception is at times greater than reality.

Australia and New Zealand were by far the worst countries to tour for home bias. In fact, although I've toured Australia on far more occasions than New Zealand and therefore have seen far more poor decisions, both playing and commentating, I'd put the Kiwis slightly ahead. That 1980 tour left a lasting impression. India and Pakistan umpires had reputations, but as far as I was concerned, nothing could top what I experienced in New Zealand.

Just allow me to be a little precious for a moment here, but how many extra wickets might I have taken had Billy Bowden and Rudi Koertzen been standing at my end in Australia and New Zealand respectively? The wickets of Ian Chappell and John Parker come immediately to mind. The ugly scenes created on that 1980 tour of New Zealand, England's tour of Pakistan with the Shakoor Rana v Mike Gatting incident and the sight of Sunil Gavaskar and Arjuna Ranatunga leading their teams off the field in Australia in protest at the umpiring might not have occurred if the independent umpiring panel had been in place. You only have to look at how few seriously controversial incidents there have been in the game since 2002 due to umpiring, to see how beneficial that move by the ICC has been. A big tick in the box for the ICC. Of course, we could go back to home umpires, thanks to the referral system, but an independent third umpire would still be required.

With the ICC paving the way for more harmony off the field and less controversy on it, the other big positive in the game has come in the players' physical and mental preparation for battle. If I had been bowling fast today, there is no doubt I would have been fitter and better prepared. Don't get me wrong, the West Indies under Dennis Waight were the fittest team around. Probably the fittest team there had ever been at that time, but it was just the beginning, the trailblazing if you like.

Before Dennis arrived on the scene we didn't know what a tracksuit was. There was no such thing as a warm-up kit. Players would turn up an hour or so before the match started and put on their match gear. Batsmen, wearing just gloves, would have a few throwdowns on the outfield and pat the ball into the boundary boards and bowlers might turn their arm over. That was the preparation for the day, especially in the Caribbean, where if nets were available at the ground, they were on the outfield so would not be prepared for use during the game.

Dennis changed all that and we went from international players who would do minimal fitness and practice (I remember there wasn't even any team training when I was with Jamaica) to guys who would work so hard and be so dedicated that people would actually get to the ground early to watch us train. When we finished, they applauded us from the field. I think they especially liked the catching drills we did. Clive Lloyd would hammer the ball at us from not very far away and catching those missiles impressed people. This was one area where the current players have nothing on us. We were intense. Dare I say it, way more so than the West Indies team that dropped all those catches at Lord's in the first Test in England in 2009. As a matter of fact, I challenge any West Indies team, post-1980s, to say they have been as good with their catching drills; hence the catching has not been as high a standard. Irrespective of any changes and advances in the game, the old adage still applies: 'CATCHES WIN MATCHES'.

Otherwise it has all moved on again since our days, for sure. In the chapter about Dennis, I mentioned the rubber bands we used for strengthening during exercises and every now and again you will see players using something similar, although now they have the option of visiting the gym either at the ground or the five-star hotel they are staying in. Players have never been fitter or stronger and that is absolutely as it should be.

Medical care has also never been better. Looking solely at how cricket has changed for the players, this has to be the greatest advancement. They have doctors and physios who travel with the team now. We just had Dennis and if there was a serious problem he would try to get hold of a doctor on the telephone or try to book you an appointment with a specialist at a hospital. If you were struck by the ball while batting (good luck trying to avoid that over a career), or perhaps in the field, then you played on. If you got hit on the finger by a lifting delivery, perhaps jamming it against the handle of your bat, the pain was pretty intense and the damage inflicted could be worse than today as the equipment wasn't as good. A bit of ice and some cold spray was the treatment and if you could hold the bat you soldiered on. There was no other option available. It was the done thing to play through. No player was keen to make a fuss in case it was seen as a sign of weakness. And if you couldn't play because of a niggle, that meant someone else would. You might not have got your place in the team back.

I remember playing a Test match in Antigua with three

broken bones in my instep. I think it must have been against Australia in 1984 because I was not diagnosed with the breaks until the tour to England later that year when I was forced to have an x-ray done due to the pain. Every time I slammed the foot down the pain would shoot through my foot and up the leg. It wasn't swollen or bruised, just very sore. The pain just would not go away and in fact nothing showed up on the x-rays until I had a barium x-ray done. I had to drink this radioactive liquid that attached itself to healing bones and showed up to reveal where the break was. It also showed me where I had broken bones previously which had healed. I'd had no idea. Of course they were just hairline fractures and in those days you tried your best to play on as best you could. MRI and CT scans are the norm for the modern player, making sure such injuries are picked up early.

The medical people with the international teams are thoroughly professional and do a first-class job of keeping the players in the best possible condition. Any hint of a problem and a full-scale investigation is launched. Quite right. It is the job of the doctors and physios to pick up on these things, so anything less would be a dereliction of duty. However, sometimes you get the impression they are too protective, which leads to some people saying the players are soft for all the 'pampering' they get. I don't necessarily share that view. Although there is now a lot more cricket being played at the highest level as a result of better medical care, careers are being extended, an overwhelmingly positive thing when you have such a short shelf life as a cricketer.

Having said that, the old fogey in me is quite pleased that I am not being subjected to all those doctors poking and prodding. A lot of the time they would have told me that I wasn't fit enough and I was someone who wanted to play all the time. For example, remember when the so-called experts told me I had 'glandular fever' on that England tour of 1976? They wanted to send me home. 'This guy can't complete the tour,' they said. Had that happened today, I would definitely have been sitting at home with my feet up because players have no say in it. The doctor's advice comes before player opinions, as it should, that's their job. But never would I have taken those 14 wickets at The Oval and who knows what would have become of my career? Phew! I'm getting in a sweat just thinking about it.

What I would have welcomed was the in-depth cricketing analysis provided by specialists who must be boggle-eyed with all the staring they do at laptops. They can tell you the strengths and weaknesses of the opposition and break it down into individual players: this batsman scores 70 per cent of his runs on the onside, so-and-so has been caught in the slips 25 per cent of the time. Fantastic stuff.

I would have enjoyed being told that sort of information about batsmen I was going to bowl at. We had our plans, of course. We would gather for a team meeting and go through the guys who we thought might cause us a problem and mull over ideas about how to deal with them. A lot of the time I would rely on my memory bank, checking it for how I, or my teammate, got him out last time. 'This guy is vulnerable outside off', 'this one doesn't like it in his ribs' or 'don't give him anything to cut'. That last example, we often found out the hard way in a match situation, instead of a boffin printing out a graph to let us know before we had even laid eyes on our opponent.

I would like to see what one of these analysts would have recommended about me. Hearsay and memory were probably the best route to go down when I was at the crease. Still, I suppose all the pie charts and percentage figures would still have told him that with my bat approaching three pounds, all I liked to do was stand there, swing through the line of the ball and go down the ground. I didn't fancy picking up the bat too high; a cutter or hooker I was not. But then again, my batting wouldn't be something they would have spent much time on.

Off the field, there have been advances in the way cricket is broadcast. This has been a major fillip for the sport. Years ago there actually wasn't that much cricket on television, and viewers would get their view of the action from one end only, from the top of a stand and with no close-ups. It wasn't until the Packer revolution that things started to change. I don't need to tell you what has happened since, but suffice to say, all the improvements have not only enhanced the enjoyment of the viewer sitting in his or her armchair, but their realisation of what exactly cricketers go through. Thanks to innovations like the close-ups, super slo-mo, snickometer, speed gun and I dare say, the stump mike, they are more in tune now with the nuances of the game and the emotions players experience. They are able to identify with them more. In some respects people have now realised what a hard and intense game cricket is.

I have a very sketchy memory of me and my West Indies fast-bowling colleagues being asked by the *Sun* newspaper on a tour to England – I think it might have been the 1980 trip – to bowl at a fridge and they would then measure the indent that the ball left. Now, I'm sure this was not to work out how fast we bowled and, my recall on this is vague enough anyway, but it must have had something to do with trying to illustrate what international cricket was like in the middle at that time against the fastest bowlers in the world. You wouldn't need a gimmick like that today.

If all the examples I have mentioned above are the good changes we've witnessed, then it's time to discuss the bad.

Firstly, walking – the act of a batsman not waiting for the umpire to give him out when he knows he is – and sledging are two of the most controversial topics in cricket. They are relatively fresh ones in terms of the history of the game. It is all down to player behaviour, which is not as good as it could be, or has been in the past. I think everybody is well aware of the fact that I have been annoyed by batsmen no longer walking. 'You would say that, you're a bowler' will be the charge against me, but hold on, batsman, bowler or specialist fielder should all be united in wanting the correct decision to be made.

Walking is now a rare sight. When I went on that first overseas tour to Australia, I was deeply shocked by the debatable umpiring and the fact that the Australians didn't head for the direction of the pavilion as soon as they had nicked it. In England it was a different story. I had become accustomed to hearing about the game in England being described as a 'gentleman's game' and when I went there in 1976, I was not disappointed. Nine times out of ten batsmen would walk and when the odd one out – if you'll excuse the pun – didn't, it was frowned upon. That batsman achieved almost instant pariah status and his reputation made the rounds.

Over the years this has changed dramatically all over the world too. It's probably the other way round now with one in ten walking. Cricketers will tell you that umpires are there to do a job and they are not going to do it for them. Others say it is a swings and roundabouts situation – one day you'll get a bad decision, the next you'll get away with one. It all evens itself out in the end.

I don't believe in either argument. What I believe in is getting as many umpiring decisions right as possible. Surely cricketers would want the same? Walking would help to achieve that. In spite of the batsman's refusal to tuck his bat under his arm and turn on his heels, we are getting closer to that. The Elite Panel has helped, so too has the referral system that was introduced by the ICC in Test matches in 2009. I was delighted when this was announced because in the interests of fairness, it is vital that you get as much accuracy as possible.

You may recall it was used on an experimental basis in the West Indies versus England series that same year in the Caribbean. A lot of people got rather hot under the collar about it because they reckoned that mistakes and blatant mistakes were being made. It seemed to be creating more confusion than clarification. Some wanted it abandoned immediately. The simple matter was that it wasn't being used correctly. But that wasn't the fault of the system. It is a perfectly good one and it is just down to the umpires on the ground, including the third umpire, to implement it correctly.

This should certainly help in getting more correct decisions, but wouldn't it be great if we could just rely on batsmen taking the decision out of the umpire's hands when they can? There is so much to gain. As a player you would benefit from your own honesty because you would develop a reputation as a walker and far less likely to be on the receiving end of bad calls from the officials. Surely it is common sense that the fewer decisions an umpire or any official has to make, the less chance of him making mistakes? This is where the game needs to go. Unfortunately players today do not see it that way. They don't necessarily want correct decisions; they want them to go in their favour whether they are right or not. This is very unfortunate.

The only players of the modern era I can recall who did walk were Brian Lara and Australian wicketkeeper-batsman Adam Gilchrist. And do you know what happened to the latter? He was virtually ostracised by his teammates for his policy. It didn't matter whether it was a big game or a meaningless one because I remember he walked in the World Cup semi-final in Port Elizabeth in 2003.

These two players were the exception rather than the rule. I have asked quite a few non-walkers about their policy. For instance, why do they decide to walk and not wait on the umpire's decision when they have driven the ball into extra cover's hands or hooked down the throat of fine leg? Their responses have been the same. It's too obvious they are out, so why stand your ground. Believe me, that's not a good answer. What it tells me is that they will try to get away with whatever they think they can. This sort of thinking is unsportsmanlike at best and bordering on cheating at worst. We have seen other more serious incidents recently of players pushing the envelope on the field to get a wicket. I believe that Paul Collingwood, the England captain, should have called back the New Zealand all-rounder Grant Elliott after he was run out while lying on the floor following a collision with a bowler at The Oval in 2008. Worse was New Zealand running out Muttiah Muralitharan when he left his crease to congratulate Kumar Sangakkara on a century in Christchurch in 2006. It's easy to defend those actions by saying no rules were broken but surely the game is bigger than that.

Those two examples are quite extreme I suppose. More subtle is sledging. Some of the stuff said on the pitch does not have a place in the game if you ask me. Okay, I'm not so naïve to think that it didn't happen in my time, but I can honestly say that it was never a policy or plan considered by the West Indies teams I played in. Nor did an opposition player direct any insults at us, which was probably wise because you didn't want to upset the fast-bowling contingent.

Sledging is supposed to have its roots in humour and banter. Yet it has clearly grown into something more ugly. One well-known captain called it 'mental disintegration'. Please. Some of what has been reported to have been said in recent times goes beyond the acceptable.

It is not pleasant to see players mouthing off at each other, particularly the way the Australian and Indian players were having a go at each other in a recent Test series. The name-calling in that match actually made more headlines than the cricket! No way is it a good example to set youngsters watching on TV. Unfortunately in my role as a commentator I often hear what is being said on the stump mic. It is switched off between balls for viewers at home, but we in the comm box can still get the feed (the ICC demand the same rules for us as you at home, but broadcasters don't always pay attention). Some of the things said are totally out of order. It is getting so bad that cricket is the new football, if you see what I mean. Football players dive and feign injury. Cricketers try to con umpires and bend the rules.

The catalyst for this unsportsmanlike behaviour by players is, sadly, money. It is not the sole motivation, but sure as hell it is at the end of the line. With the game money-mad, there is more pressure on players than ever before to win a match. It is the win-at-all-costs attitude that is eroding standards. It doesn't have to though: golfing standards haven't fallen as prize money has escalated.

I would say that the ICC has tried to clamp down on sledging. They have made a pretty good job of it, too. The Code of Conduct has reined players in somewhat and the umpires are stepping in every now and again.

I suggested once at an ICC cricket committee meeting that umpires should have red and yellow cards to dish out to badly behaved players. Obvious attempts to mislead officials – I'll stop short of calling it cheating – should warrant a yellow card. Of course my idea was never taken up, but if cricket is becoming more and more like football, why not adopt some of the rules that FIFA has implemented to make things fairer?

It all comes down to that magnificent saying, 'It's just not cricket', which is known around the world and was even once used in a speech by Kofi Annan when he was head of the UN.

It stands for fair play and if a less than cricket-mad country like Ghana, where Mr Anan is from, knows about its meaning, then why has the cricket world forgotten?

So that is the good and bad dealt with. Don't worry, I haven't forgotten the ugly . . .

21

THE FUTURE

If Twenty20 is the greatest change the game has seen, then I believe it also poses the greatest threat to its bedrock – Test cricket. I have genuine fears for the future of the five-day game. And if there is a question mark over that, there also have to be doubts about cricket in general.

Twenty20 was conceived in 2003 in England, where a domestic league was set up. The ECB hoped that it would provide a much-needed cash boost to the 18 county teams, while the pundits and supporters thought it was all just a bit of family fun. After all, it wasn't proper cricket; batsmen tried to hit the ball out of the ground as much as possible and bowlers were reduced to being cannon fodder.

Even back then I was not a fan of it. I thought it was gimmicky and was an example of cricket dumbing down for the masses. But even I would have been surprised if, in the first year, someone had said to me, 'One day, players will choose to play this over Test cricket.' But then again I would not have envisaged the amount of money being thrown at the shortest form of the game.

That is exactly what has happened. As mentioned earlier, in 2009 a captain of a leading cricket nation said that he wouldn't be upset if Test cricket died and that he preferred playing Twenty20. Although Chris Gayle tried to play down the comments later when he realised the furore it had created, he only said what others are thinking and probably haven't been brave enough to say.

Earlier that English summer, he had arrived two days before the start of West Indies' first Test against England at Lord's, having stayed back later than originally planned to play a match for his Indian Premier League (IPL) team. That was not right; the rewards for that extra game had clearly come first. Dwayne Bravo, an all-rounder, didn't turn up at all. The West Indies Cricket Board received a medical report to the effect that he was injured and not fit enough to play Test cricket, so didn't pick him for the tour, but allowed him to go and play in the IPL. If he was fit to play in the IPL, why was he not playing for West Indies? Is playing in the IPL that physically easier than playing Test cricket? The number of cricketers who have reported various injuries coming out of the IPL season would suggest the contrary to me. Another question: if there was no IPL, would Dwayne Bravo have toured the UK with the West Indies team? I'll have to try to bite my tongue here, but you get my point about players pushing Tests to the back of the queue.

It is not my intention to use Chris's words to criticise or belittle him. It is his opinion and he had every right to say what he thought and I repeat, there are probably others who think the same but don't say it. In a way, we should be thankful for hearing what he had to say because he has highlighted exactly why cricket's future could be very dark indeed. Thanks to the emergence of first, the Indian Cricket League, and later, the Indian Premier League, which started paying out huge sums of money for players – the signatures of Kevin Pietersen and Andrew Flintoff cost an incredible US$1.5 million each – the importance of Test cricket is being diminished.

Players have taken their eye off the red ball, instead being captivated by all the trappings the white ball offers. You can't blame them. It is a short career and if a guy gets the opportunity to go for the jackpot contract in India instead of working his socks off in the five-day game where it is far harder to make an impression, then obviously he is going to take it.

I have no problem with Twenty20 being part of the cricketing landscape. We have seen that there is enough interest around the world to justify it and it can work quite comfortably alongside 50-over games and Tests. There is enough room in the calendar for all of them if structured properly.

The problem is the money and greed that surrounds the domestic Twenty20 leagues. If players continue to be attracted by the mighty dollar, then 50-over and Test cricket will suffer. It is these two formats where the players build their reputations, particularly Test cricket. Players are nothing without Test cricket, and initially the ICL and IPL made a beeline for the Test players because they were the most famous. For an obvious reason – their appeal to the masses – the objective was to sign the big names whether they were suited to that form of the game or not.

The eventual team selections in some cases demonstrated this. You had a great Test player like Glenn McGrath not even able to get a game for his team in the IPL in the second season, and Paul Collingwood, a decent Test batsman, was only asked to carry the drinks. If that isn't a big negative, then try this. How many cricketers have brought their Test careers to a premature end when the clear choice became evident: represent your country or go for the big bucks in India? It doesn't say a great deal for Twenty20 as it is structured now. Nor will it do much for the longevity of Test cricket.

So what can we do? The debate has been fast and furious. And it is continuous, with no real answers so far. Some say that 50-over cricket is finished and that it should be discarded. I don't agree. There are even a few saying there is no need for Test cricket as there are too many draws and it's boring. They couldn't have watched the first Ashes Test in 2009 at Cardiff if they're of such opinion and that's just a recent example; there have been many others.

There is a far more simple solution. The ICC need a kick in the backside to make them wake up to what is happening in the game they are supposed to govern. At the moment the ICC is guilty of the serious crime of not doing its job. They need to start paying more than lip service to safeguarding the future of Tests, try to slow the gold rush in domestic Twenty20 leagues and, the old chestnut, play less but more meaningful cricket.

It sure is a challenge, but one that must be won. So let's start here.

The ICC officials talk a load of hot air about the sanctity of Test cricket. They talk the talk, but don't walk the walk. If they were serious about keeping Tests sacred, how can they stand by and allow a Test cricketer to earn X dollars per year while a Twenty20 guy earns XXX dollars?

I am fine with Twenty20 bringing money into the game so long as it is distributed fairly, but the consistently skewed earning power between the two inevitably means that people will choose the shorter game. We need one big pot that the money goes into and get it distributed fairly, comparable across the formats. Either that or the IPL, which at the time of writing seems more likely to survive than its counterpart, the ICL, must be found its own space that conflicts with no international commitments. The ICC need to stand up to the Indian Board and money men and make it happen because you will never see those domestic tournaments clashing with India's international commitments. Not one Indian cricketer has been faced with the choice of the IPL or their country.

The ICC may say they don't have that sort of power. I don't know their constitution, but if this is correct, it needs to go and have a word with FIFA. What would be even better would be for the BCCI (Board of Control for Cricket in India) to accept that there was some damage being done and work with the ICC and other cricketing boards around the world to solve the problem. I tire of reading certain comments from the sub-continent, chastising anyone who says negative things about the IPL. The usual comeback from India is that it supplies the majority of the money available to the game, the power base has now changed and the rest of the world had better accept the situation. How did England and Australia behave when they had all the power, they ask? To that, I say this: a few may not agree, but one of the greatest men to have walked the earth in my lifetime is Nelson Mandela. He and his people suffered tremendously under the apartheid regime, but when he took over the mantle of governing South Africa, he did not vin-dictively return the favour to the opposition, which would probably have sent South Africa into chaos and terminal decline. Instead he charted a way forward that started with forgiveness and inclusiveness, bringing about a smooth trans-ition instead of possible revenge and bloodshed. Maybe some folk in cricket administration can learn something from the great man.

Giving the IPL its own space would do a great deal to help Test cricket. As would the ICC and certain other admin-istrators getting it into their heads that what Tests do not need is a gimmick to be attractive to people. They reckon one way to save it is to play day-night Tests? Have you ever heard of anything so ridiculous? If I wasn't laughing at these guys, I'd be crying for them.

What a great idea to devalue Test cricket further by playing a day-night version where the conditions change in a matter of hours under lights. And they wanted to trial it in England of all places, where the switch in conditions is greater than anywhere else in the world when the sun disappears and the floodlights come on. Whether real or perceived, cricketers believe batting in daylight is far better than under artificial light, whether the ball is red, white, pink or any other colour that they manage to come up with.

This is not about coming up with the wackiest idea. It is about doing the basics. You know what, if a ten-day Test match was taking place with the greatest players in the world on show and across the road there was a Twenty20 match with run-of-the-mill players, it is the Test match that would attract the biggest crowd. Keep the big players happy because that is who Joe Public wants to watch. The actual format or rules of Twenty20 are not the reasons so many people have watched it. Sure, the shorter time frame is important to some, but it is the big-name players who pull in the crowds. You only need to look at England's domestic competition for proof of that. In the first year it was a novelty and the crowds were good, but now they are dwindling because, guess what, there aren't enough big names.

Mind you, the ECB has completely lost the plot regarding Twenty20. They have seen how much money it can make and have become greedy. They had scheduled a second domestic Twenty20 competition, calling it the English Premier League, although at the time of writing, this tournament is unlikely. Thank god for that. This, folks, is a very fine example of discovering the goose that laid the golden egg and then killing it by making it work overtime.

This leads me nicely back to the amount of cricket played, which surely must be reduced. This is absolutely vital for the future.

Test matches are fantastic sporting contests with two sides joined in battle, each trying to give the other a good beating. It's great theatre and is the reason it is held in such high regard. Lately it has been more of a pantomime when you have countries playing each other when one has not even a hope of drawing, let alone winning. I mean, how is the public supposed to feel a sense of anticipation about a Test match between Australia, the highest-ranked side in the world and Bangladesh, the bottom-ranked team? It can't. And I use those teams as an example because of their relative strengths at the time of writing in 2009; obviously it could be two other teams at some other juncture. Yet the ICC is asking these countries to play each other home and away every four years. Crazy. As things stand right now, Test cricket is being devalued by some of these encounters.

When I was with the ICC cricket committee, I wanted to see certain teams, which had Test status but played to the standard of associate members, lose their full membership. But surprise, surprise, it didn't happen. There were certain countries that wanted the status quo to remain for political reasons. You see, full membership allows certain privileges like a vote on issues coming in front of the board, and certain votes could not afford to be lost. It is all political.

Okay, it hasn't happened and more than likely never will. But there are other options. At the moment the ICC has ranking systems for both Tests and ODIs. Why not use those rankings to determine two leagues within each discipline? The Future Tours Programme is then scheduled from the top six teams, which play each other home and away within the same four-year period, but only have to play the other teams below the top six once, maybe at the home venue of that lower team? This would ensure more meaningful Test matches and preserve the integrity of the game at the highest level. It would also ensure less cricket. It would ensure interest when the supposed minnows, for want of a better term, take on the big boys. Gate receipts would be guaranteed and there would be no loss of television interest because the minnows would be playing at home. The teams below the top six would also have their Future Tours Programme within the same four-year period, and of course there would have to be a promotion and demotion system worked out so that as countries improve and others deteriorate, there is an interchange.

Such a format would raise the bar for standards. Sides would be continually testing themselves and the competition would improve. English county cricket eventually went that route with two leagues, which has created more interest in games right until the end of the season in September. And it hasn't detracted in any way from the teams in the second division; they haven't fallen away and been forgotten – just have a look at the England XI and see how many are from teams in the second division, including the captain.

It would get the fans excited again. And once you have captivated their imagination, the cost of a ticket to go and watch these games should be slashed. Test crowds are down the world over because of the amount of games played, and in some countries the amount of money the fans have to fork out for a day's entertainment adds to the mismatches. In England, clubs are perceived to be protected from the dwindling numbers because the small grounds are pretty full with 10,000 supporters in, but when you only have 10,000 in the MCG or Eden Gardens, you know you've got a problem.

When the attractions of Test cricket are considered, ticket pricing is hardly ever discussed, but it's an important factor. It doesn't represent the best value in the world to go to watch a Test match on one day: you are not seeing the whole game and in these harsh economic times, food and travel on top of your ticket makes it an expensive experience. Think of the parent going with their other half plus one or two children. No wonder people choose Twenty20.

If the ICC was serious about saving Tests, it should strongly advise the home boards to do more in terms of ticket pricing, such as special offers for the whole family to go and watch the game. Come to think of it, the individual boards should have the common sense to institute it themselves.

Although there are many arguments against Test cricket, one big positive that Test cricket has over the other forms of the game is the revenue generated from television. If you ask any television company which generates more advertising revenue, Twenty20 or Tests, they will tell you the latter every time. The exposure a company's product gets is far greater in Tests, whether they are advertising on television or through a boundary board. In the IPL, a 'strategy break' had to be introduced into the game after ten overs to run adverts so that advertising revenue could be enhanced.

Rest assured I was not watching any of the IPL. Nor was I tuning in for the World Twenty20 Cup in the summer of 2009, in which the West Indies reached the semi-finals. I decided to go abroad for the two weeks the tournament was on. Apparently during one game my Sky colleague Michael Atherton, commenting on West Indies opening the bowling with two medium-pacers, exclaimed, 'Thank goodness Michael Holding isn't here, what would he make of it?' I think Athers knows what I think of Twenty20, and knows that I wouldn't care one iota! I am not going to support the form of the game in its present format and structure.

I suppose if you believe that a country's performance inTwenty20 is worthwhile, you could say that West Indies did well. But it was entirely predictable that the players showed more gusto in that competition than in the Test series in England that same year. Many eyes from far afield were focused on the Twenty20 and it wouldn't be farfetched to assume that most players would have been hoping to catch enough attention to ensure future appearances in the lucrative IPL. You get the feeling that some of them would have taken to the field with injuries that would have kept them far away from any final XI for a Test match.

The subject is getting me down, so let's move on. But I will finish with this: if the ICC does not step in to redress the balance in the world game, then cricket will be downgraded to something which only makes money, rather than a sport. Surely it would be better if it were to be known as a money-making sport?

22

FACTS AND FICTION

When I started planning the chapters for this book, I had no intention of writing this particular piece, but during the summer of 2009 I got so sick and tired of some of the nonsense spouted about West Indies cricket that I decided to set the record straight in black and white. 'West Indies can't play spin', 'West Indies can't play swing bowling', are two of the lines rolled out over the years whenever we have failed against one or the other. Absolute rubbish. I have tried to ignore the comments over the years and move on, but enough is enough. A famous saying is that statistics are used like a drunk uses a lamppost ... for support rather than illumination. But boy, am I going to shine a light on the truth and send all these people who peddle these lazy clichés scurrying for cover.

I find it intensely annoying when commentators make these comments without having done any research. It does a disservice to themselves, the people watching at home and, of course, the nation or player they are discussing. One of the reasons they do it is that it can just be the easy thing to say and I thought this happened a few times in the summer of 2009 when West Indies were thrashed by England. I have no problem admitting we were well beaten, but it was for a different reason to the one that some of my colleagues advocated.

When the sides met in February 2009 in the Caribbean, a lot of people were talking about the impact Graeme Swann,

England's spinner, was having. He bowled well, taking 19 wickets. When he picked up one of his victims, we would often hear suggestions that West Indians had never been good players of spin bowling. A few months later in England we heard the same thing when Swann took a wicket. And if it was a swing bowler who claimed one – swing bowlers James Anderson and Graham Onions took 21 between them – well, that was because West Indians have never been good players of swing bowling. On both counts it is untrue.

The spin myth was spun back in 1988 when Narendra Hirwani, the Indian legbreak googly bowler, bamboozled the West Indies batsmen in Chennai. His brand of spin claimed 16 wickets in that Test match and suddenly everyone seized on the supposed fact that an Achilles' heel of a fine West Indian side had finally been exposed. The media had been waiting for such an opportunity and they could barely hide their delight. Since then, whenever a spinner gets wickets against the West Indies, the line is just thrown out there: West Indians are poor players of spin. So consider this. Of all the countries to tour India, widely recognised as the place that offers most assistance to a relative army of spinners, West Indies have the best record.

Our first tour there was in 1948, which we won, and between then and the turn of the century, West Indies visited India another seven times and won four of those tours. So in all the West Indies won in 1948, 1958, 1966 and 1974, dropping only two Tests out of 18. The only defeat we suffered was the six-Test 1978–79 series when West Indies were depleted by the ban on World Series players. It was only 1–0 as well. When we went there in 1983, it was business as usual and we won 3–0, India's heaviest defeat since our 1958 vintage had despatched the hosts by the same margin. The tours of 1987–88 and 1994–95 were both drawn series.

How have the other countries fared in the period from 1949

to 2000? Well, we'll start with those sides which the experts consider to be much better players of turn than West Indies: Pakistan and Sri Lanka. Between both countries, they have toured a total of 11 times to India for Test series, Pakistan six and Sri Lanka five, yet they have only one win between them and that came from Pakistan in 1986–87, a series they won 1–0. Sri Lanka have never even won a Test match in the country, having played ten in total. In our study period, Australia have won four times in India, but before their previous success in 2004, they had not won in four series, a run stretching back to 1969. England have won two series (I am not counting one-Test series played by these two established sides, so therefore England's Golden Jubilee Test win in 1976 doesn't constitute a series in my book. Sorry!). New Zealand have never won there. South Africa have won one of their four series.

So that's one fable laid bare. Now for this swing thing.

It would be churlish of me not to admit to West Indies playing the swing bowlers poorly in England in 2009. But to say that has always been the case is misleading. What I would ask is this: what country doesn't have a weakness against swing bowling? They all do because it is tricky to bat when the ball is hooping around corners. In the Ashes series of the same summer, Australia were bowled out cheaply every time the ball started to move. And England were blown away for 102 at Headingley when it started to swing.

Headingley is world-famous for helping swing bowlers, so you would reckon that with English batsmen being able to counter it with such expertise, they would have a very fine record there. Not so. It is their second-least successful home ground. West Indies have won there six times, a record which makes it our joint-first most successful away ground with The Oval in terms of Tests won. The WACA at Perth and Adelaide Oval are next best with five wins.

I loved bowling at Headingley and I had a chuckle to myself when Sir Ian Botham, the king of that venue thanks to his heroics in 1981, gave me a gentle ribbing that I never pitched the ball up. I responded with, 'If you want to drive Beefy, rent a car.' Well, a friend heard this on commentary and uncovered some stats showing that of my 249 Test wickets, 33 per cent were bowled. Of Beefy's 383 Test wickets, only 15 per cent were bowled. Of course Beefy was only joking so no harm done, but back to the original point of West Indies and swing . . .

West Indies first won a series in England in 1950. Of the next 11 series up to 1995, West Indies won seven of them and drew two. Perhaps on each of those nine tours there was never a cloud in the sky and the ball steadfastly refused to swing. The fact of the matter is that the quality of players decides whether a team can play swing or spin, not where they're from. When England had good players they could play swing or spin. When West Indies had good players we could do the same. Currently, the West Indies are not blessed with huge talent, but please let us not all have such short memories.

It is upsetting that such baseless comments keep cropping up. However, I am used to West Indies cricket being run down. When we were at our most successful, the credit was far from forthcoming from most of the international press men and the establishment. With our battery of fast bowlers, they said that we were ruining the game with slow over rates, boring cricket and intimidating bowling. The funny thing is, while such sections appeared to loathe us, the people that really mattered, the fans, loved us. If we were so bad for cricket, why were there packed stands whenever we played abroad? Why were supporters from the host country so keen to see us play, and most likely, win? And as mentioned in another chapter, why did we manage to turn around so many fans into supporting us instead of their home team?

Perhaps the critics got riled because we often would triumph in three days and it would cost someone a load of ticket revenue! Naturally I say that with tongue in cheek, but the hypocrisy of it all gets to me. In England in the summer of 2009, Sky ran a feature about how wonderful a sight it was to see Lillee and Thomson running in during the 1970s, bowling short, breaking bones and hitting poor old David Lloyd in the box. It was a great sight (sorry Bumble!), but I remember watching it and thinking, 'When we did it, we never got this sort of romantic reaction.'

You would have to ask the press guys why they were so against us. There were many and shall remain nameless and they know who they are, but one will be named in David Frith. Personally I have never had a problem with this gentleman. In fact, I have hardly had any personal interaction with him, but when you're writing in *The Wisden*, considered pretty much the bible of cricket, I think you've got to be fair-minded and objective and the following account didn't convince me of that. Frith, former editor of *The Cricketer*, founder of *Wisden Cricket Monthly* and well-known journalist, was most vitriolic in his criticism of the West Indies pace attack and the way we went about our job. His opening salvo before the West Indies 1991 tour of the UK was the following. 'Another invasion is upon us by a West Indian team that is the most fearsome, the most successful and the most unpopular in the world. Their game is founded on vengeance and violence and is fringed by arrogance. The only mercy is that they're not bringing their umpires with them.' Followed later by: 'These matches have long since become manifestations of the racial tensions that exist in the world outside the cricket ground gates.'

These attacks by Mr Frith weren't restricted to the 1991 tour either, as between 1977 and 1991, there were many instances of negative pictures of West Indian fast bowling in the *Wisden*

Cricketer magazine's limited pictorial section with some very unflattering captions. I wonder if, with all that has gone on in the game since, he still thinks he was justified in his utterings or if he has a tinge of regret about some of those articles of old? Could it have been jealousy, the fact that some were not too keen on a nation of just five million producing so many good cricketers and proving to be so successful?

Sadly, I think some areas of the press secretly enjoy that West Indies cricket has slumped. Quite a few will publicly decry the decline, but it's only lip service, crocodile tears. Privately they'll be quite happy. I can tell you now that if West Indies cricket was to 'die and the body cremated', there would be few obituaries in the international papers. It would be 'sad' and then they'd move on. In fact, in recent times with the West Indies going through their woes, there have been articles written suggesting that the West Indies team as we know it should be disbanded and the individual islands go it on their own. I know those pushing this plan would rejoice if it did go ahead because it would mean no team from the Caribbean could ever be world champions or hand out the kind of beatings the West Indies have done in the past. The individual islands just don't have the population or resources to cope, and that is what they would hope for. What outweighs all this negativity is that I know the people that mattered, the real cricket fans, enjoyed our cricket and we are very proud of that fact.

Anyway, that's off my chest. And cathartic it is too. I have no plans to do another book after this one, so I wanted to make sure that I said everything I wanted to. As the title says, 'No Holding Back'. I am making these notes as Laurie-Ann and I prepare to leave Newmarket for the winter and head back to the sun of Miami, Jamaica and the Caribbean. I make my escape every year from England just before it turns chilly and I can look forward to walks on the beach, barbecues with friends and family, and of course, taking the odd call from Sir Michael to talk cricket and horses. I won't be working on or watching much cricket though, instead developing my burgeoning interest in American football. When you get to understand it, it's like chess, the nuances and the tactics.

Fear not, I am not about to try to reinvent myself as an American football commentator. I will be around on Sky Sports for a few years to come yet. During the Ashes summer, I was offered and signed up with Sky again until 2012. I am delighted that they will have me and it will be a pleasure to be invited back into people's living rooms. So long as you'll have me, of course.

INDEX

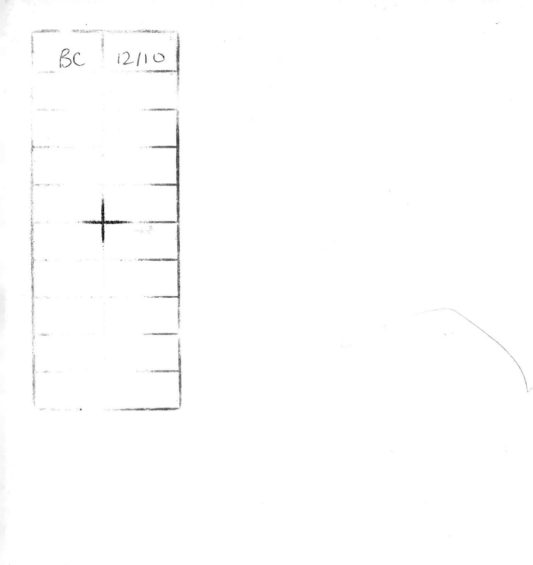